Praise

A Cage Full of Monkeys

This is not just a memoir but a work of art. A brilliant, poetic storyteller, Souza relives his California life through uniquely filtered lenses. His memories, his imagery, his character portrayals, his emotions are vivid, intense, and sometimes seemingly surreal. In *A Cage Full of Monkeys*, we feel transported back in time while in an altered state.

—DAVID ARETHA, award-winning author and editor

This personal narrative by Richard Souza is both wistful and insightful as it weaves in childhood memories, youthful explorations, and later-in-life awakenings. He reveals key events not in the chronological pattern common of memoirs but by connecting the illumination of insights gained through unwavering excavation of a long life. From his youthful days in California as a competitive roller skater through recent years witnessing his mother's decline and death, Souza reflects on how time distorts memory but also distills the past into its most meaningful essence.

—JULIANNE COUCH, author of *Searching for Here: Mapping an Unfenced Life*

I'm dazzled by the beauty of your writing and your evocative reflections on your life and the power of memory.

—MARTHA BULLEN, Bullen Publishing Services

The first awakenings of human longing beautifully told. So elegant. There is only ever one childhood for each of us, and within each child comes the struggle to adapt. This memoir, from beginning to end, is written as if to be read aloud.

—FRANK TROIA, artist

In *A Cage Full of Monkeys*, Richard Souza takes an unflinching look at childhood sexual abuse, unrequited love, and the care of a parent with dementia in gripping, elegant prose. Set against the backdrop of a conservative small town, this is a gay coming-of-age story unlike any other.

—Douglas C. Haldeman, PhD, professor, John F. Kennedy University

A Cage Full of Monkeys filled me with so many feelings. It's all there—love, courage, empathy, wonder. I have never been affected like this by anything I have read. It is so visual, like watching a film or a great play. I can't stop weeping.

—Jackie Bruni, PhD, family relationships

A vivid exposure of the soul. Passionate. Brilliant.

—Elisabeth Miller, university professor, educational leader, teacher

I opened the first pages of *A Cage Full of Monkeys* this morning and finished the book this afternoon. I loved it, it struck home, and I cried at the end.

—Gene Zaphiris, editor and publisher

As an aspiring writer, I am always fascinated by how good authors are able to put their thoughts into words in a way that makes readers engage with them, to experience their senses, to share their joy and pain, to see the world from their eyes. Your writing accomplishes this beautifully. You have a gift for poetic prose, and the steady rhythm of your style never ceases to entice the mind. Your writing is both interesting and inspiring, a somewhat rare combination these days. After writing something I consider to be poignant and well-phrased, I continue to struggle with gnawing questions: *How is my reader going to react to this? Is this important to write about? Does this even really matter?* My opinion is that you have mastered these questions for your readers, and the product is a beautiful book.

—Chris Liles, writer and educator

Mr. Souza is a brilliant writer and wordsmith, and his work belies the fact that he is a first-time author. He slides through his memories and revelations with ease and takes us on a journey of self-discovery, sharing some very intimate details about growing into his adulthood as a gay man. Some passages are funny, some are sad, some relatable, some not . . . but if you grew up in the 1950s, you can certainly see some familiar backdrops to your own life or some strong parallel lines showing we are all human, not monkeys in a cage. Perhaps that might be the point of his book. Most poignant was the last chapter—his mother dies, and he attempts to answer his own question: "Part of me still asks why I write this. Is it so that I am not completely, irretrievably, irreversibly irrelevant and invisible in the way that most old people are?"

—DONNA JOHNSON, artist, fotografia U S A

When offered the opportunity to read *A Cage Full of Monkeys*, I hoped for something more than a "coming of age in 1950s California" saga and was not disappointed. I was presented with this thoughtfully chosen and ordered chronicle of memories, presented as a subtly layered collection of tactile experiences, conscious sensations, and sometimes unexamined perceptions. The writer maintains both the cohesiveness of his storytelling with a sensitive awareness of the people who were a part of his experience and his ability to move beyond emotional perception and present a solid descriptive environment for places and events when necessary.

The author presents a tableau that moves us through a series of life-defining experiences . . . from the beautiful five-year-old walking down his driveway to visit a neighborhood friend, to the first devastating rejection of unrequited young love, and on to the perhaps unknowing but courageous high school teacher who presented Walt Whitman to his '50s-era students. The memoir moves beyond youth and into maturity and a reckoning with mortality in the all too familiar overrated high school reunions and the all too real, and raw, details of parental aging and death.

This is an arresting and evocative read, and, as good reads often do, it leaves us with unanswered questions, not about the resolution of events in the story but about the essence of life itself . . . "Isn't it possible that the experiences we recreate reflect the truth and at the same time keep us from it?" One question answered by Mr. Souza is that this memoir is indeed a coming-of-age tale. And it is quite clear that *coming of age* is always a work in progress, never complete until we reach "beneath the flow of time closer and closer to that place where the first and last moment of your life meet, compressing into nothing."

—RICKA SMITH, research consultant

The book is brilliant and witty. I loved the poetic picture you present, as well as the correlation to other writers, poets, films, and/or references to music of the period. I particularly enjoyed the symbolism. The book has a flow and certainly is very engaging.

—ISRAEL GARCIA, school administrator, educator

Souza has managed to write a memoir that reads like a novel. It is indeed a "remembrance of things past" but with a modern twist of a young boy growing up in a rural Northern California town, struggling to understand his sexuality during the politically and culturally conservative 1950s. The town comes alive, as do the characters and his compelling struggle to harness memory to connect intimately with the journey of his heart.

—KAREN RANDALL, English Studies Chair for the Schools of the Sacred Heart, San Francisco (Retired), recipient of the Herbst Foundation Award for Teaching Excellence

A CAGE FULL
of MONKEYS

A MEMOIR

RICHARD SOUZA

A CAGE FULL of MONKEYS

A MEMOIR

Saudade Publications

A Cage Full of Monkeys: A Memoir
Copyright © 2021 Richard Souza

Published by Saudade Publications

Paperback ISBN: 978-1-7367597-0-7
eISBN: 978-1-7367597-1-4

Cover Design and Interior Design: GKS Creative
Project Management: The Cadence Group
Copyediting and Proofreading: Kim Bookless

To Mom and Dad

That I could have shared this with you . . .

CONTENTS

I BOUGHT MY FIRST PIECE OF "SERIOUS" ART (above) when I was in my twenties. It was titled *Woman in a Fur Coat,* painted in 1964 by Nathan Oliveira, an artist associated with the Bay Area Figurative School along with painters such as Richard Diebenkorn,

David Park, and Elmer Bischoff. Oliveira was at that time represented by Gump's, a high-end store in San Francisco that had an art department on the third floor. The artist was teaching at the California School of Fine Arts, now the San Francisco Art Institute. I was working in Alturas at the far northern tip of California as a grade setter on one of my father's road construction jobs and had seen the painting on a weekend trip to the City, as San Francisco was—and still is—referred to by locals. Not *Frisco.* Ever.

At $675, I couldn't afford the painting and left the City with this mysteriously provocative woman haunting me. I couldn't stand it. Her face kept reappearing in my head. A few days later, on my lunch hour, I called Gump's from Alturas, spoke to the manager of the art department, a Mr. Dana Reich, and made arrangements to buy the painting via installments, paying seventy-five dollars a month for however many months it took. I have followed Oliveira's career ever since, acquiring a handful of his works as money would allow.

One Christmas when I was in my sixties, I was given a biography of Nathan Oliveira by Mike Dunham, the same friend who had been a student of the artist and who initially introduced me to Oliveira's work. The book analyzed his haunting figures in relation to his life and heritage—Portuguese, the same as mine—and added a new word to my vocabulary, one that shed a dazzling light on the story within these pages, resonating in the same provocative way the paintings themselves did. The word was used only once in the text: "(Oliveira's) isolated early life, together with the traditional Portuguese sense of *saudade*—meaning yearning, melancholy, grief, and sorrow—accounts for the nature of much of his work . . ." Seamlessly, this insight fit into what I was writing.

Hauntingly, the word kept resurfacing in my mind, as the *Woman in the Fur Coat* had.

This led me to research, first to the dictionary: "Saudade (singular) or saudades (plural), pronounced [saw'dadi]: a feeling of nostalgic longing for something or someone that one was fond of and who or which is lost. It often carries a fatalistic tone; a vague and constant desire for something that does not and probably cannot exist: a turning towards the past or the future; the love that remains or the love that stays after someone is gone, particular to the Portuguese." In a page of this book, I quote Edmund White, who touched on this feeling in his own way, writing of it as "the exquisite melancholy of parting." I would add that it's also when the heart tells you there is something more.

I now see *saudade* in feelings I've never understood, ones that are carried in the blood pulsing through my veins, passed to me from my forefathers, like dark eyes and swarthy skin, born within the Portuguese consciousness in the same way some are born with ESP.

I get validation of its existence every time I'm in Portugal. I see it in the architecture. I hear it in *fado*. It's in the faces on the street and the voices filled with rain. And I see it every time I look at *Woman in a Fur Coat*. It is and always will be somewhere in my cage.

PREFACE

I'VE LIVED MY LIFE TWICE. The first, day after day, mostly in a predictable routine with events as unremarkable as the terrain of the moon. The second, and perhaps the more significant, is how I remember those days, since remembrance is the second round of living life—special events, relationships, memories I've lost or refuse to let go of or those that seem not quite mine to remember, the way dreams beg to be forgotten. Or ones that have so utterly evaporated they might never have occurred. Parts of life, even the most memorable, even the most beautiful, can eventually slip away. They fall into dark corners like pearls from broken strings and are scattered, gone because you stop looking for them.

The way remembering moves time backward, if only briefly, is continuing what no longer exists—of having conversations that never took place or, if they did, having been reinterpreted over time, redescribed in new detail and thus, as Proust believed, become all the more real. Often, when I reach back, when I stretch long and hard for the past, the memory comes back lifeless and fallible. But when it comes involuntarily, it is full of life, perfect, timeless, extraordinarily vivid, things I haven't thought of in years but having been as firmly embedded as knots in wood.

The past is unseeable in its entirety, knowable only in the parts that come back, each with a version of what the whole might be. So, isn't it possible that the experiences we recreate reflect the truth and at the same time keep us from it? May we be unwitting casualties of perception who, through our own sensibilities, filter and arrange and rearrange the world—day by day, relationship by relationship?

It is throughout this process, laced into the pretzeled shape of thought, that memory intercedes at will, often with a thick consistency into which you may sink, like a bog or murky water that runs on the river bottom. It is undefined space, no light to guide you and, more than anything, is silent. No one hears it. Not even you.

Memories might appear as a presence, an outline, a sound, a name or a face I once knew—loved, even. Or sometimes just a vague thought that hovers, like a figure with wings that draws near, attaches briefly, then withdraws. Something that was, or nearly was, or wasn't at all, perhaps replacing what is real and tangible with an image so clear, so bright, it seems as if its arms are reaching out, needing to be embraced.

They offer comfort, these things I speak of. These shadows. These ghosts. These friends. Also, pain, like the phantom sensation of a severed limb. Sometimes fused with regret but sometimes with the possibility of resolution, as if visiting the past reopens and repairs itself simply by looking a second time, or a third, understanding in a new way, even though what recurs is less an accurate snapshot than it is an impression of what was or what could have been. Not a photograph but a painting—like Monet's water lilies.

This premise has led me to two truths: the truth of each day as I lived it and the truth of how that day, and all of those that followed, is remembered and misremembered. As hard as I try to resurrect events using that most sensible corner of my heart, I can't help but wonder if, over the course of a lifetime, I have reshaped experience from the real to the surreal. Looking backward from the far end of life, nearly eighty years, this could be true. I can't know for sure. Nostalgia, *saudade* too, may have painted romanticism into experience in the same way Monet's brush painted impressions into water lilies. The past, as well as being the soul's deepest possession, carrying the most intense colors of feeling, like the purples and blues of those floating flowers, is already written. But is the ink completely dry?

These pages are my water lilies laced with a lingering recrimination: it has taken too long to paint too little. Although, as for that, how can a life be told in one telling? How can one story explain all the people in it? Similes and metaphors, after all, only approximate. Nothing is really like, or as, anything else.

My story, as I tell it, is a variation on a memoir and not propelled by form or format. Events and recollection came to me without a clear beginning, middle, or end, although within the loose narrative, there are flashes of each. As my life went from page to page, the emotional, intellectual, and spiritual "I am" wrote itself.

By the end I find it's a mood piece, reflective, with no steady build to an ultimate climax. The conflict is even and pervasive. There is no arc, no crescendo that tidies up the finale, tying it into a neat bow. Bittersweet feelings run through the pages like a low-grade fever. There is no antibiotic for nostalgia. There was no escaping my *saudade*.

Important people in my life do not always receive the space in the story they should—many important relationships I had as an adult are held in reserve for another time, another place: Ken, with whom I had a lifetime friendship; Laurie, with whom I came close to matrimony but walked away; Betty, a high school love that was never resolved; others. Some appear and disappear in my mind, never finding a place on the written page, even though I take great pleasure in what they were to me, a pleasure more complicated than mere affection. They all had ramifications on my life I could not have possibly imagined at the time, all having made up the artifacts of my difference and my sameness. They all deserve complete chapters, if not entire books. Here they may occupy only a paragraph or less. You will want to know more about them. Not this time. Maybe in a sequel, or from novels of their own, as yet unwritten—ones of hope and anticipation, of disappointment and triumph. Strangely, some of the figures in these pages found a way to influence my narrative to a degree I do not fully understand.

I have rarely spoken about what you will find in these pages and have never written about it until now. Just know that what I say, apart from how it is said, is not always sequential, and it covers a period as wide as birth is to death. In this indulgence of the heart, I discovered the journey of remembering is a long one, and during its course, water lilies floated and drifted as flowers on the water would.

CHAPTER 1

THE HOUSE
ACROSS THE STREET

THE THRUST OF RECOLLECTION begins on a Wednesday, a July day in my hometown of Yuba City, California. It was 1946. I was five and an only child for what seemed like forever until my brother, Ron, was born seven years later. I remember my mother asking me when she was pregnant and near delivery whether I wanted a baby brother or sister. I also remember my answer. "I don't know," I said, not sure if, after always having been the center of attention, I wanted it any other way.

I started life as the firstborn of a second-generation Portuguese-American family, nonpracticing Catholic on my father's side, heir to his rich heritage of humble beginnings. My paternal grandparents, both from the Portuguese Azorean islands, made up the émigré fiber of America in the early years of the twentieth century, coming through the confusion of Ellis Island and eventually making the small, rural Sacramento Valley town of Yuba City their permanent home, never relinquishing the cultural habits and mindsets of the Portuguese. Grandpa Souza was a quiet man whose physical presence somehow affirmed to the observer that he could fix anything than was broken and do it without expectation of recognition or applause.

My younger brother, Ron, and me, circa 1948.

It was rumored that he was the strongest man in three counties. I believed this when I watched him walk out of a burning farmhouse with his arms wrapped around a refrigerator, carrying it down the steps safely away from the fire. Although he never learned to read or write, he was successful as a farmer, a father, and a grandfather. Grandma Souza was the woman of family firsts: first to have a television set, black-and-white and then color; first to have forced air heating and refrigerated cooling; first to hire a professional interior decorator to do her house, first to own a mink coat. And she was the best cook in the family. The Souzas flourished in the community, solid and well-respected. It was from this background that I inherited the brooding, darkly romantic tendency that intensified the agonies and ecstasies of just about everything in life—a blessing and a curse I have learned to live with.

On my mother's side, the heritage was rich and humble in a different, fundamentalist way, Christian and benign, but benignly stifling, as only Nazarene beliefs can be. These grandparents came from the Depression-era drought and the parched Dust Bowl of the Midwest, one of tens of thousands of migrant families who came west. With four young children, three girls and a boy, and whatever they could carry, they traveled in boxcars, as hobos would, to the promising land of California. Prior to this exodus, my grandmother—Nannie, we called her—had been courted at age fifteen by two young men, Vess Davis and his brother. She loved the brother most, but being a pragmatist by nature, Nannie married Vess, whom she did love but a little less, because he had promised her a house, a promise the other brother couldn't make. Times were tough.

I never knew Grandpa Davis. He died when I was a baby, leaving his wife and children and forty acres of peaches which she continued farming for the rest of her life while giving herself over to God completely. Her convictions were as firmly closed as a clam, and so devoted was she that she built, or helped build, three Nazarene churches in her lifetime. For her, Moses had literally parted the Red Sea and the earth was absolutely created in six days. "And God rested on seventh," I heard many times. But the Christian beliefs of her church—and to a lesser degree, the Catholic influence from the paternal side of my family—were inconsistent with something I felt but at first did not understand. Nazarenes could not dance, play cards, or go to movies for fear of eternal damnation. Few Nazarene women wore lipstick. Sin was everywhere, in every nook and cranny of life, as menacing as a cigarette tossed into dry grass. Salvation was in giving your existence over to Jesus and praying for those who did not know Christ. To me, the heavy religious mumbo-jumbos of both religious doctrines were hammers of lamentation, whips of prohibition cracked over the heads of the entire world. The more religious I tried to be, the less certain I was about myself; to accept the teachings of the Bible, so much of the "I am" had to be stifled, buried deep, to satisfy God's word. To be welcomed into the fold, I had to ignore who I was.

But intuition proved stronger than what Christianity offered, pearly gates aside. By the time I entered high school, I had managed to distance myself from the church, unable to abide the repression and a hypocrisy that is epidemic today, as seen in the irrational, sometimes rabid and cruel evangelistic arm of Trump's religious right and in the monumental coverup of sexual abuse in the Catholic Church.

I showed promise as a child. My mother gets the credit for this, having given my education an early start by teaching me numbers and the alphabet before I entered school. Each afternoon, I would sit on her lap while she leaned over me, lovingly guiding my young hand into numbers and letters of the alphabet using the columns of yesterday's newspaper as my writing pad.

This daily ritual of making scrawly letters and numbers created a world, a realm, out of a piece of paper and a pencil, smelling the mother-smell and feeling her mother-warmth. She read me to sleep, fixed my breakfast, wiped my butt, took my temperature when I was sick—all things that involved touch. Touch. Critical to a child and bonding me more to my mother than to my father. But not unnaturally so.

I could count to one hundred and write my first and last name the day she took my hand and walked me up the steps of the Bridge Street Grammar School in the fall of my fifth year. The advantage I had by then, perceived as precocity by the school, started my formal education as a first grader, a year ahead of my age group, skipping kindergarten and casting me, then and thereafter, as the youngest in the class—grammar school, high school, and college.

It was during this time, before I could properly read and write, a series of events took place that would stay with me all my life. They became the initial force behind this story. On one particular day, I became much older than my years.

A metal cash register, enameled bright red with five pennies in the change drawer, is the first thing I remember my father giving me. I was four, an age where the implication was not within my reach, the shape of its meaning clearer over time. I watched and listened. From as far back as I can remember, I was encouraged, aimed but not pushed, toward the world of business. My father was present in those early years when many fathers weren't. World War II raged. Farmers were exempt from service. The nation had to eat.

Dad loved the outdoors and made fatherly attempts to engage with me on that level, thinking, or perhaps hoping, I would be inclined in that direction too. I wasn't. A fine athlete in high school, he had been scouted by major baseball teams before the war, but farming and family came first, dispelling those aspirations. I had inherited some athletic ability, in an arena that would be discovered later when a talent I had surfaced at the age of nine. By then, the playlist of father/son activities had been exhausted. Hunting, fishing, throwing a football—none held any appeal.

Fishing was an interminable act of waiting. Sometimes for nothing. I'd been fully outfitted in equipment from Ray Gauge's Sporting Goods Store—waders, camouflage clothes, an olive drab cap, and twelve-gauge shotgun that was heavy—for my one and only duck hunting experience. That, too, was like fishing, but very early in the morning in the cold and the fog—more waiting, now in a dreary duck blind. In the warmer days of fall, pheasant hunting was the thing, but, sadly, it was more of the same. My lack of enthusiasm was clear, and my father's largesse didn't press the point. I don't know if he was disappointed or relieved. I was the latter.

The approach to business was a different story altogether, and I took to his example well, quickly grasping an important principle: when I agreed to do a job like water the lawn, pull weeds, clean the garage, etc., I negotiated how much I would be paid.

Generally, my father laid out by example what he saw as the terrain of a good and proper life, for himself and by extension for me. I thank him for that. But the ideology, the geography of life as he saw it, lived it, and presented it, seemed flat and unsatisfying. Something in his version was missing. It had nothing to do with him but with a growing uneasiness somewhere within me.

Fantasy became as much a part of my emotional makeup as reality. Movies offered more information about life than life itself. Images on the screen were bigger than life. They taught me to imagine, and instilled a sense of wonder, a desperation almost, that needed satisfaction. Movie theaters were big empty spaces then, not the multiplexes they are now. They were enormous black voids where make-believe clicked frame by frame, so fast everything disproportionate in black and white was more real than the colors outside. In the darkness of the elaborately appointed cavern, with its heavy velvet curtain and fading gilded frescos, I could become more myself, as my psyche became other-sided.

My parents were accomplices, unwitting ones, in this transformation that was happening to me. They loved the movies too. Once—and sometimes twice—a week, we would cross the bridge that spanned the Feather River and connected Yuba City to Marysville, stand in the ticket line that was always long, wrapping around the corner of the block, finally taking our seats in the State Theater with its gilded spectator boxes lining the walls, uninhabited spaces from the bygone days of live performances.

There were double bills in those days—two movies for the price of one—from Sunday through Tuesday, with the program changing Wednesday through Saturday. I can remember my parents letting me attend the movies alone while they went out to dinner—horrifically unthinkable in today's world. At age seven, I saw *Mr. Peabody and the Mermaid* a total of ten times, sitting through the film twice in a night and being picked up by them in front of the theater afterward. Waiting, I would watch the big, black Gyrinidae, whirligig beetles, entertained by their scurry and crackle, some flipped on their backs, legs flailing frantically, until our car pulled up in front.

Beautiful people and magical stories had infinitely more appeal to me than hopscotch and catch-ball and jacks. Passion for art and music and literature would come later, but, as a child, my chosen portal into the world was through movies, an obsession bordering on addiction that only grew stronger as I got older. Sitting by myself in the first row, crushed by the images, oblivious to the outside world, I fell into every trap a story could set, losing myself in the labyrinths of fictitious people and worlds.

Unnoticed then, the thread of an outsider running through me created distance, not only from others but from myself—from my feelings and impulses, leading to a private fantasy life in which I felt special, separate, and apart. From the silence of genetic lines buried somewhere deep inside, a personal upheaval had also been born, one that pulled me in a different direction, away from the world of business and my family's culture of silence. It was as if an amorphic second self lived inside me, parallel and purer than the one I visibly inhabited, one that came with noises in my head, my voices, a cage of monkeys, some friendly, some not, loud and screaming or muttering indistinctly, sending me into moods of melancholy that I kept to myself, guarding these feelings as I would if they were important secrets. (Did I conjure the voices? Or were they entities of their own?) My parents never knew or even suspected the conflict within me, inclinations taking shape that even I could not identify much less address. Neither worry nor concern was ever expressed in their eyes or in their voices. I was the first-born son. I was perfect.

Approaching the peculiar and uncomfortable task of describing myself—my physical appearance in particular—I have to pause. What *did* I look like? I suppose it's fair to say my face was a combination of contradictions. It occupied space on a head that was too large for the body, starting at the top with a loosely drawn widow's peak that framed a deep, wide, typically Portuguese forehead that seemed to further diminish an already diminutive nose. Full, fairly pouty lips exposed, when I smiled, some crooked and misaligned teeth. Thick eyebrows I knitted together, often in doubt or melancholia, influenced the intensity of my bittersweet chocolate eyes from which similarly colored eyelashes swept up and away in an unnatural length and curl, so much so that ladies of a certain age were often inclined to comment on them, even stopping us on the street and bending down to my level, the smell of their intoxicating perfume raising my face up toward them, marveling at the bright-red lipstick and heavily applied rouge. "My word," they'd say. "Wherever did you get those eyelashes?" As bashful as only small children can be, if I answered at all, I would say, "From my dad," staring hard into the sidewalk with a tight smile. The features added up amounted to a dark-complexioned child who was, sadly, almost too pretty to be a boy.

My father was as handsome as a movie star. He was in equal measure a man's man and a lady's man, a quality he wore easily and well. My mother, quiet and more reserved, was the perfect complement to his magnetic bluster and radiated the wholesome beauty of the Oklahoman Midwest where she had been born. At a glance, I was a combination of these well-matched, attractive people. Threaded through me was my mother's quiet nature and the deeper, less stoic impulses of my father, ones laced with *saudade*.

On the day that begins this accounting, the day that is the most vivid of all my childhood memories, a door was thrown open and I discovered how emotions, seemingly incompatible with one another, existing side by side in the same human heart in what was an extraordinary experience for a boy of five. It was a pivotal moment, and, as with many of life's turning points, this one coalesced not in an instant, but over the course of a number of days.

It was eleven o'clock in the morning and already hot. It would get hotter still, becoming another scorching day in a long line of one-hundred-degree days. There had been the usual number of late spring showers but none heavy enough to damage the peach or prune tree blossoms or knock the rice down. A long run of hundred-degree temperatures was what the farmers hoped for this time of year. All crops in the valley were doing well, especially the rice crops that thrived in the heat—the hotter the better. Grandpa Souza had started farming rice the year I was born, 1941. Without fanfare or intention, I would become the third leg of a three-generation rice-growing operation.

"Everybody's sayin' the rice is lookin' pretty good this year," my father had said at the dinner table, a comment coming, as many did, from out of nowhere while he was trying with some difficulty to cut his well-done pork chop. "Everybody" meant his farmer friends. What they really meant, but would not say in so many words, was that they thought we were in for the best harvest in years. A farmer's superstition prevented them from saying so, just like the Chinese who would repeat, "Bad rice, bad rice," when the crop looked especially good, diverting the rice god's attentions to other matters.

I walked across the street from my house to the Reeveses', went up the three steps to the front door, and rang the bell, the sun in the pale sky beating down, promising more heat. The temperature had taken the form of nervous, upward spirals that made the asphalt seethe as if it were a living thing. I was already in a sweat, a consequence of summer temperatures in the Sacramento valley but more to the point, from my anxiety, which was running higher than usual—for good reason, as it turned out.

As I'd crossed the street, three stiff metal slats of the Venetian blinds in the front window popped down into a "V" for a second or two and then snapped back into place. Bobby was watching and, as I interpret it now, the sharp, furtive action may have indicated that he shared the same anxiety I did.

The shades and curtains in the rest of the windows were closed. For insulation from the heat? Maybe. For privacy? That'd be more like it. The family sedan was not in the driveway, so I knew Mr. and Mrs. Reeves were both at work. Bobby was there alone. *Good.* Being around grownups I didn't know broke me out in a sweat. A lot of things did. I'd met his parents when the family first moved in, but I can't say I knew them. Nor could anyone else in the neighborhood. They were odd but not in a way I'd seen before, never attracting attention but unusual in ways most people wouldn't notice. Except me. Movies (and my voices) gave me a keener antenna than other kids my age for anything out of the ordinary.

As I came down the driveway, old Mrs. Hurlbert, our next-door neighbor, was bent over pulling weeds in her rose bed along the low picket fence that separated her yard from ours. Wiping the sweat from her forehead with the sleeve of a housedress I'd seen her in the day before, she looked up and uttered in her usual way, annoyed about nothing in particular and everything in general, "Whew! Hot enough for ya ta-day?"

Because of where I was headed and what I was about to do, I was feeling pretty full of myself—for reasons that will become clear—in spite of my anxiety, and I crowed, "You bet, Mrs. Hurlbert. Hot as hell."

For a moment almost too brief to notice, she was speechless, lifted eyebrows and stiffened shoulders the register of her surprise. Unlike adults, cussing was not something I did except here and there in extreme circumstances, but always under my breath and limited to *hell* and *damn*.

I crossed the street and walked up the steps to the house. At the exact moment I rang the bell, I could feel the feathery sense across the nape of my neck turn into beads of sweat that rolled down the middle of my back. Before the dual tone of the chime ended, the door opened about a foot, quickly but stubbornly with a jerk and just wide enough for me to slip through if I turned sideways. I didn't think anything of it at the time. There was too much other stuff on my mind—the what-ifs and voices all arm wrestling one another. From the opened door, I could hear the monotonous din of the swamp cooler rumbling low and cautionary in the background, its cool air a welcome hit from the heat outside. Come afternoon, the rooftop machine would be scant relief from the unmerciful late-day sun. But in the moment, the whoosh of cool offered some measured relief that seemed to go hand in hand with the invitation I'd received a few days earlier.

"Come on in, buddy," Bobby's voice said from behind the door. There was a slight tremor in those four words—a noticeable contradiction to his usual confident presentation. I found this not only oddly comforting but somehow provocative too. Turning sideways, I stepped through, not realizing this skewered entrance would, by the end of the day, also skewer my life and my approach to just about everything I thought and did. Sidestepping grew into a pattern of not only avoidance but survival.

———

As I said, they were odd, the Reeves family. A few weeks earlier, when the moving vans pulled up across the street one afternoon and the contents were unloaded, the three of them settled in quickly with none of the normal neighborhood interactions. No "Hello, I'm Mrs. So-and-so," over the back fence. No borrowing a cup of sugar. No coffee in the mornings with the neighborhood ladies. And no one had been invited inside. A couple of other things were odd too. Within the first few days, Mr. Reeves planted geraniums—red ones, a couple of dozen. He placed them randomly across the front of the house, and down the driveway back to the garage with no apparent consideration for design or logic. Within days, weeds started sprouting around them, as if they'd already been forgotten. This was a clue of some kind. But what? That they really didn't plan to stay? Or maybe, a house isn't necessarily a home? Plus, the doormat was blank. No "Welcome" or "God Bless Our Happy Home." Nothing. Which seemed to be a message in and of itself. It made me wonder. Getting to know neighbors had always been easy until the Reeveses showed up.

Neighbors got to know one another in 1946. It's what people did. Neighborhoods were trusted places—safe, small, self-satisfied communities within themselves. Car doors and backdoors were left unlocked. Only the Bank of America building in Marysville on the other side of the river had a real, bona fide, wired-in security system. Nothing was remote-controlled. *Remote* was a place, or a possibility,

13

not a device. A bowl of ice set behind a table fan was an invention. Beer cans were opened with a church key. Letters were written by hand. Computers, email, smartphones, and all such technology were generations away. Only birds tweeted. People said things like, "What's the diff?" instead of "What's the difference?" And silly women were called "ninnies." Expressions like, "He gives me the heebie-jeebies," were commonplace. All of a period piece now.

Money loans were made on the strength of a single signature, and sometimes just a handshake was your solemn oath that, in my father and grandfather's day, was as good, if not better, than a written contract. We lived simple lives in flat towns where blocks were laid out in confident, symmetrical lines with streets free of litter, and houses were painted white or other optimistic colors. Everyone knew which street led where, and there was just enough town to go around. Families were convention-bound, held together by everything rose-colored. The world inside their houses seemed like good places, places in which all the damaged pieces somehow fit.

The clatter of glass bottles on Tuesday and Friday mornings announced that the milk was being delivered to your back porch. And in good weather, the ice cream truck jingled, crawling through the neighborhood every afternoon with popsicles in different colors and ice-cream-filled 50/50 bars. Most ailments were treated with aspirin or mustard plaster, and people knew America was the best place on earth.

It was a time when I was still fascinated by the world, not yet aching for the world to be fascinated by me or by the symphonies I would orchestrate, the great book I would write, and the classic performances I had yet to stage. There were as many heroes in real life as

14

in Hollywood. And for the price of one ticket, the State Theater, my dark refuge and world of fantasy, offered up the Movietone News, the Looney Tunes cartoons, the previews of coming attractions, and sometimes a sing-along following the bouncing ball. Studio trademarks—the roaring lion, the statue holding the torch, the radio aerial with electricity pulsing from it—preceded the feature movies, all of the above stimulating my imagination and, like mold on an orange, covering the curvature of my mind. Movies held the intrigue of other lives, foreign to mine, where couples met in shadowed places and unlikely stories paralleled reality like dreams, never intersecting it.

It was a time when the anticipation of what life could offer was as rich as Grandma Souza's bread pudding, the thought of tomorrow a richness in itself, and each individual day seemed like happiness itself where bad things could only happen in nightmares or accidents. Hope was lofty and, as Emily Dickinson said, "a thing with feathers." Butterflies skimmed the grass, uncountable masses of red-winged blackbirds swirled in cloudless skies, and possibilities blossomed far in every direction, as far as the dream in your eye could take you.

Home, honor, and a good work ethic, pretty much in that order, were valued qualities that were instilled and practiced. Small towns were theme parks before theme parks were corporate investments, before there was reality television, outlet malls, and fast food drive-throughs, and before morbid obesity in children and adults was tacitly accepted. On warm summer nights, dusk settled on Brown Avenue, the lights in the houses came on one by one, and behind the closed doors, everybody was content. Or so it was assumed.

But home for the Reeves family didn't seem to be any of these things. It veered from the norm in the most subtle of ways. They went

15

to work every day, Monday through Friday. Nothing odd about that. But for some reason, I harbored the suspicion that the three of them might pick up and leave at any time with no goodbyes and as little fanfare as their arrival. This is what they eventually did.

They were cordial enough in passing, and, if someone came by, Mr. Reeves liked to hold court in his own greasy way on the sidewalk from time to time, lurking around outside his house as he often did; the missus smiled, with reserve, and nodded, but always from a distance. Interaction with other folks didn't go further than that, at least not according to the whispers I'd overheard.

On the surface they appeared to be a regular working-class family, nothing more, nothing less. Mr. Reeves wore a brown suit every day and carried his brown briefcase when he and his wife climbed into their late-model sedan, drove off in the morning, and came back in the afternoon just like lots of other people, the neat routine in line with the widely practiced work ethic. But I was curious about them. I dwelled on their comings and goings more than I normally would. That was the kind of kid I was. And at the root of my curiosity was a fascination with their son, Bobby.

Initially, it was Mrs. Reeves I found myself studying. I gravitated toward the company of women, even though Roberts Sr. and Jr. had more imposing physical presences, each extreme in different ways. But women were more interesting. They talked about things I liked. And they smelled good.

Mrs. Reeves was just this side of homely. "Not much of a looker," I'd heard it said. She was plain but comely, like a well-groomed female sparrow, always dressed in a tailored outfit or a nondescript housedress: never any frills, very little color, some shade of beige as a rule. Next to her husband and son, she faded into the background, becoming almost invisible. When she left for work in the morning, she wore a single strand of pearls over a freshly ironed blouse, but that was the only jewelry I ever saw on her except for a wedding band worn thin, I supposed, by the habit she had of endlessly rotating it around her ring finger with her thumb. Her hair was fine like corn silk except, like her posture, it seemed tired, lank. And was a color I never saw on any color sample at Arne's Paint Store. When she looked at me, she seemed to be on the verge of saying something. But she didn't or couldn't or wouldn't.

There were no physical attributes to connect Bobby to his mother except for one quirky detail, here and gone, almost too quickly to notice. It was there for a second and then gone, like she had caught herself in a secret she felt guilty about, something she felt compelled to hide. It was in her eyes, not the color or shape but at the back and at odds with the rest of her. It flashed to the surface from time to time when she tilted her head a certain way, or when watching her son or staring at nothing—an emotional wound, perhaps, a scar that crisscrossed the inner workings of her mind. Once she caught me looking at her, and a smile registered on her face—complex but fleeting. It was this mysterious quality that pulled me to her, never to reach her, never even to know her first name. She is a blurry figure to me, like some unidentifiable face in the third row of an old photograph.

The Reeveses' triad remained a source of imagined stories I told myself over the years, bizarre combinations of fact and fiction weaving the family into macabre fantasies. When, as an adult, I read Tennessee Williams's lurid short stories, *One Arm, Hard*

Candy, Desire and the Black Masseur, I mentally constructed wildly speculative theories about the Reeveses—many of them sexual in nature and going far beyond events I could have had no plausible insight into, unable to share the wild speculations with anyone but myself and my voices.

———

The first encounter with Mr. Reeves I have memory of happened one day when he stopped me on the sidewalk as I was pulling my red wagon home from the park. My recollection tells me it felt premeditated, as if he had been waiting for just the right opportunity.

"Hey there, young man. I've been wanting to meet you. And you call me Bob now, ya hear? None of this 'Mr. Reeves' stuff."

He oiled his hand into mine, a grip tight enough that I immediately felt subservient, holding it long enough that something inside told me it was inappropriate, but I didn't know in what way. His eyes locked on mine as he leaned into my face, smelling of Lucky Strikes and stale breath, his look steely, his voice as seductive as Pastor Jackson's, the preacher at the Nazarene Church in Hallwood we went to, absent the ejaculations of "Amen" and "Praise Jesus" followed with "Amen" and "Praise Jesus" coming from the congregation. There had been speculation that "Bob" was, in fact, a Holy Roller preacher. He fit the profile. And Mrs. Reeves would have made the perfect preacher's wife. But their car was always in the driveway on Sundays, so that was that.

Bobby inherited his good looks from his father. Had they been the same age, they might have been twins, sharing predatory lips and penetrating eyes. But time had erased all but the most general similarities. Bobby's youth and the beauty that went with it had long since vanished in his father, now egg-shaped and turning gray. In its place, however, was a powerful replacement—confidence in a body language that was as cocksure as it was unnerving.

Their smiles were still identical. They both had good teeth. Perfect and straight. The smile itself immediate and effortless. But there the similarity ended. Mr. Reeves smiled when there was nothing to smile about, flashing his teeth like a light bulb, flickering and twitching as if it were about to burn out—a contradiction that held your attention and confused your thinking. A troubling wheeze pushed air through the stiff nose hair like wind through dry weeds, as if something vexing was gnawing at his insides trying to get out. And his eyes betrayed thoughts he kept to himself, as disturbing as his handshake and bad breath. He was a double entendre before I knew what double entendre was.

"I have to go home now, Mr. Reeves," I said, pulling my hand from his and crossing the street to the surety of the other side, the silence of my departure punctured by the noise of the wagon wheels on the asphalt.

To this day I still ponder the psychological makeup of the Reeveses, as individuals and as a family. They were in my life so long ago and for such a brief period. How much of what I remember is real? How much imagined? Or misremembered? The interminable voices in my head created doubt then. They still do.

"Now remember, no pancake ain't so thin but what it ain't got two sides," my grandmother would say, underscoring the point with pursed, thin lips, narrowed eyes, and wagging finger. It was her way of saying there are two sides to every story. (Convolution of the English language was typical of that side of the family. Double negatives were their specialty.)

In reality, Mr. Reeves may have just been a slightly odd man with oily hair and sweaty palms working at a humdrum job, with a humdrum wife, living a humdrum life who, produced an outstandingly beautiful, charismatic son, about whom you will hear much more. This could be the other side of the pancake. Or Mr. Reeves could have been fumbling around in some kind of unmentionable sin, living a sordid life of who knew what, leaving the same kind of emotional claw marks on others as he did on me, marring whatever came near him. Which raises another question: Did tendencies of the father also lurk in the psyche of the son? *The sins of the father.* Or were the Reeveses just a little odd?

I have never been able to put Bobby into a specific category or define him as he really was. It was too long ago. My superlatives were too meager then, my adjectives inadequate even now, despite the fact he was so pivotal in my life and around whom memories revolved for so many years. More than someone in the past, in his own way, he was also of my future.

Physically, he could have stepped directly off the silver screen and, from that glittery place, exuded a presence that was as intimidating as it was dazzling, but unlike the ambiguous male beauties of the 1940s and '50s—Tyrone Power (who, people said, looked like my father, or vice versa), Farley Granger, Montgomery Clift—nor the rugged all-Americans, such as John Wayne. Bobby's good looks were his own brand—original, classical, and contemporary. Bernini might have fashioned him from translucent marble. Mary Renault captured Bobby better than I ever could in a letter characterizing a

Macedonian conqueror in an ancient stone artifact. He was "a blazing sun below the horizon, not yet quenching the stars but already paling them." That was Bobby.

———————

"Bobby tells me he'd like to have you. Over to the house, I mean. One of these days," Mr. Reeves said, stopping me cold on the sidewalk. The insinuation, shaded as it was, didn't register at the time. It was hard to know what exactly he meant beyond the nervous smile tacked crookedly onto his sentences. But later that week, it became clearer when an invitation was thrown at me from Bobby himself, startling me in the much same way his father's comment had.

It was a late morning, and he was on my mind. I obsessed over him in the same way I obsessed over attractions that drew me to beautiful male characters in movies. And he looked and acted every bit the movie star, exceptional in every way, more so than anyone else I had known.

Thinking about him took up many waking hours—too many to be good for me. But thinking about him was what I was doing while watering the front yard on the day he first spoke directly to me. The lawn had been newly planted, needing soaking several times a day in the heat, a job to which I had been assigned, one of several jobs around the house I was charged with doing. Being five didn't excuse me from chores. *Work builds character*, a principle my parents believed in and lived by, *and makes you goal oriented*. I am doubtful the principle extended to one particular goal I had set for myself: get to know Bobby Reeves.

I was waving the hose back and forth slowly in square grids, my finger carefully pressing on the hose so that it put out an even spray and did not miss any fledgling grasses. At the same time, I was wondering how, and if, we could ever get acquainted. What did I, a scrawny five-year-old, have to offer someone who could ride a bike with no hands? After all, he was fourteen—practically an adult. (The difference in years, his to mine, was monumental then. And daring. After age fifty, the same difference would seem insignificant.)

And, as things have a way of happening when you don't expect them to, at that moment, with my back to the street, a voice came from behind. I didn't have to turn around. I knew who it was.

"Hey buddy, wanna come over tomorrow? I've got the new Superman comic. We could read them." (He must have realized at five I couldn't read yet. Did he even know my name?)

I turned. Bobby was pedaling his blue Schwinn in a circle in the street as he watched me, waiting for my answer. I had the presence of mind to pay attention to the voice inside my head saying, *This is exactly what you want. Don't screw it up.* Every other kid on the block would have given his eyeteeth or his best aggie for such an invitation. The mind works that fast. Like the shutter of a camera. *Click.* I was at the threshold of something big. I knew it.

His invitation might seem inconsequential on the surface. But this was not just *some* kid. It was *the* kid. Every boy in the neighborhood had some degree of fascination with him for reasons that may or may not have been the same as mine. I can't speak for them. We were young. The young fascinate easily. The truth is, although I try to articulate now what the attraction was then, I don't know for sure. That would come together later. All I know is that he commanded attention like a magnet attracts metal. He was fascinating. There was Bobby. And then there was everybody else.

This personal invitation was a coup—unquestionably a one-up-manship on the Stevenson brothers, Edgar and Tom—all vying for Bobby's attention and favor. Who didn't want to be friends with Bobby Reeves? I knew they would be green with envy.

"Just stay calm," I said to myself even as the adrenalin had started pumping and my heart beating as if trying to burst out of my chest. Then I had an idea. I'd do something I'd seen in a movie. I shifted my weight to one hip as if giving consideration to the offer and deciding if I was available. I kept watering the lawn in the same even cadence. But when I turned around with my answer, what came out of my mouth was complete and total gibberish.

"Er, uh, yeah, okay, I guess," gushed out like pent-up water from an unkinked garden hose, each word tripping like a fool over the next. I closed my eyes, clenched my jaw, and cringed. *Damn! Maybe he didn't hear.* He wheeled past me a second and third time, the grin on his face saying otherwise. Crimson crept up my neck and spread across my face. The hose had not moved, and I had effectively washed a rut in the lawn.

"Great. Eleven, okay?" he said, clearly amused.

"Er, okay," I muttered.

"Okay. See ya tomorrow," he said, breaking the circles he was making. He disappeared down his driveway and into the garage.

That's when the voices in my head, those that were with me always, started. *What a dope! That all you could come up with? Er? Uh? Yeah? What a dumbbell! Stupid!*

He caught me by surprise. I was nervous.

Nervous? You practically peed your pants!

At exactly eleven o'clock the next day, I navigated past my brief encounter with Mrs. Hurlbert, who had stooped back to her weeding, still muttering to herself. I crossed the street, glancing furtively over my shoulder. After I entered the house, the door closed behind me with a quiet but firm slam. We stood in the entrance in silence, neither of us knowing what to say. We just stood and stared. *You absolutely could be Superman!* I thought as I stood closer to him than I had ever been. Every part, every detail, seemed bigger—bigger than life itself. Just like on the screen.

He flashed his familiar smile, the one with all the perfect white teeth, which broke our stalemate, and said, "Hotter than a whore outside, huh? Gonna be a scorcher." His voice had the deep resonance of an adult. Locks of thick, curly hair, deep auburn and as intricate and detailed as Velasquez's rendering of lace, tumbled loosely down his forehead, which was uncharacteristically dotted with tiny beads of sweat. I stared, long and hard, not really able to process what I was looking at, my eyes trying to take in and record every detail. He must have heard my heart beating. It felt that loud.

We stood face to face with him towering over me, his feet spread slightly apart and his hands on his hips in the well-known Superman pose. His whole body glistened with illuminating perspiration. He was poised and ready for the hot afternoon ahead, completely naked except for the worn-out white athletic socks that fell loosely in relaxed folds around his ankles. I somehow knew I was no longer just a part of his fawning audience on the sidewalk. I was in a different place entirely.

CHAPTER 2

SWAN DIVE OFF
THE HIGH BOARD

B
RIDGE STREET WAS ONE OF TWO MAIN ARTERIES in Yuba
City. It ran east and west and dead-ended at Second Street
and the levee that held the Feather River back in winter. I
have no idea what happened to First Street. Washed away one stormy
year, I suppose, by rising floodwaters before the levees were built to
fight the raging river waters of January, February, and March. On
the other far end of Bridge Street, the west end, close to the edge of
where city met country, Brown Avenue crossed Bridge Street. Brown
Avenue was where we lived: 680. It was a new but modest part of
town, as modest as Yuba City itself, with several blocks of newly
constructed, thirteen-hundred-and-fifty-square-feet, stucco, two-bedroom, one-bath houses that have long since been discarded into the
dustbin of architectural design.

Where Bridge Street met the levee was the old part of town, the
dead-end part of town. To the right on Second Street were two blocks
of business buildings. The courthouse and hall of records, buildings of civic pride and cultural ambition, made up the original town
center. On the two blocks after that, the first residential area, were
stately, two-story Victorian houses of moneyed families, aristocrats

with names—the Winship House, the Cress House, the Swenson House—that looked down their noses at passersby of lesser station, even though some of these once-majestic homes showed peeling paint around the edges, cracks in the foundations, the settling of a corner. Prosperity does not always endure through generations.

Beyond these architectural beauties, Second Street segued into the Garden Highway and curved into the outlying farmland.

A left turn at the dead end took you under the train trestle, the entrance to the old bridge, the Garden Highway Nursery, the SPCA, and a gravel road that ran diagonally up and over the levee to the river bottoms where the Yuba City Municipal Swimming Pool was built, erected as part of FDR's many WPA projects. The swimming pool was our destination on the day I am about to describe.

On the left side of Bridge Street just before you reached this decisive intersection was our interim stop: the Toot-N-Tell-Em, the only drive-in diner in Yuba City in 1946 and the best example around of what is now commonly referred to as retro. Three other drive-ins—Shan's, Andy's, and the A&W Root Beer—appeared in the early 1950s, but none was quite as special as the Toot-N-Tell-Em with its unique waitresses—"carhops," they were called then. In this case "carhop" was a misnomer. The waitresses came and went from diner to car and back again on roller skates. They dressed in brown and yellow (Yuba City High School colors) gabardine skating skirts (very short), and in the cases where booty was generous, not long enough to cover the buttocks they bounced upon. The food was diner fare—burgers, fries, shakes, and the like. Nothing special, except it did taste special at the time, that time before fat and sugar were taken off the list of major food groups.

As the named implied, honking your car horn for service was protocol, unlike the drive-in restaurants that came later where honking was frowned upon, a sign of impatience.

"What'll it be, folks? Same as usual?" the carhop chirped to us, the handkerchief in her blouse pocket fanned out like a big "hello." Mom looked over at me. I nodded. The carhop smiled. "Burger, tomato, mayo only, fries, Cherry Coke. Right?" She looked at me and winked.

"No lettuce or onions," I added, "or anything else. Just the tomatoes and mayonnaise." (I couldn't, wouldn't, eat lettuce. The only place pickles belonged was on the Thanksgiving table in the divided dish next to the pitted olives.) Nodding, she popped her gum, making a noise like a cap pistol, and jotted the order down in waitress shorthand on her little lined pad.

"And you, hon?" to Mom.

"Just some iced tea, please," my mother replied.

"Sure nuff. Be right up," answered the carhop, and the pencil disappeared halfway and at a sharp angle as she shoved it somewhere in her cylindrical pompadour and skated away, the accordion pleats of her skirt in a bounce against her bottom.

I knew full well there would be no swimming on a full stomach—a thirty-minute wait, minimum. Mom was very strict about this one thing. No exceptions. "You'll get a cramp."

After lunch, I squirmed and fidgeted, impatient to get into the cool water from the slippery, sweaty, Naugahyde seats of the hot car as Mom ran a few errands.

The swimming pool lay in the broad, gently curving river bottoms like a rectangular but uncut aquamarine, a glistening piece of costume jewelry, its setting made of local river-run rock. The clarity of blue water was intensified by the reflecting sky overhead, striking an assertive contrast to the unpainted concrete blocks of the drab pool building and the dusty barbeque pits dotting the picnic area, with rusty grates stuck in their blackened bellies.

Nestled against the high side of the levee, the pool hugged the riverbank at the base, hidden like a secret from passersby on the city side, visible only momentarily by traffic up on the bridge to and from Marysville. The dusty gravel access road, easy to miss if you didn't know it was there, was flanked on either side by thistle bushes and foxtails all around and in between, a tinderbox ripe for a spark from a cigarette flipped from a car or a hobo.

From the top of the ridge in the sunny opening, the pool sat amid tall cottonwood trees that buttressed either end and shaded the periphery. Beyond the trees, impassable thickets. Like dandelions, snowy tufts released themselves from the trees, drifting aimlessly in lazy air, some settling quietly onto the pool and some onto the river nearby that slithered south to fork with another tributary headed for the delta.

Bobby's startling invitation wouldn't come for a couple of days yet, so I was not aware of any connection between my visit to his house and the events that took place at the swimming pool on this one afternoon. Now I can look back and see the connection. The episode at the pool was a piece of the larger puzzle that made up the entire drama to unfold in the months ahead where everything revolved around Bobby Reeves. And me.

I was already in the shallow end of the pool dog paddling in my water wings when he arrived. Not so much arrived as made an entrance. My mother sat on the edge not too far from me with her legs dangling in the water, taking some sun, and cupping water in her hand and tipping it down her shoulders and arms. Kids splashed and screamed, churning the water like a tub full of frantic sardines. The more accomplished swimmers attempted laps that were regularly interrupted by neophytes on collision courses coming from all directions.

Teenaged girls, dressed for swimming but with no intention of going into the water, lay on towels, oiled to perfection in the latest Rose Marie Reid bathing suits from Bradley's or Jay's. Teenaged boys strutted around them, combing and re-combing their Brylcreem hair, trying to look cool and trying where possible to catch some cleavage—any that Ms. Reid's designs might allow,—which, as I remember, wasn't much in those days. Parents monitored the underaged, the under-athletic, or those simply not to be trusted for one reason or another and gabbed amongst themselves in the shaded areas behind the wire fence. They drank Cokes and ate sandwiches and watermelon from red metal ice coolers whose sweat-like condensation trickled down the sides and into the grass.

The PE department at the high school had already gotten wind of "the Reeves kid" and the athletic potential there, especially Coach Rice, who had taken a summer job at the pool as the lifeguard. The coaches and staff from both sides of the river all sniffed around in June, July, and August, trying to find and recruit new players for the coming season's football, basketball, and baseball teams. From his lifeguard station at the pool, Rice had a bird's-eye view of everything except the inside of the locker rooms, which he checked out from time to time, a curious part of the job that always made me stop and wonder, one of those questions that stayed in the back of my head unasked. How anyone could drown in the locker room was a mystery to me. There was the shallow chlorine footbath. That's all. Adult thinking sometimes escaped me.

Older by probably twenty years or so, Mr. Rice was, like Bobby, lean and muscled, but similar in other less obvious ways as well. He seemed very quick to take charge, to size up a situation or an individual, and had a natural understanding of whatever stood in front of him, a talent that would have been useful in many ways, getting this job one of them.

When Bobby emerged from the locker room, heads turned. This was not unusual. He was a rare, sleek animal, confident in that way I had seen only in movies but never in real life. He was hard to miss in that red bathing suit: a tight composition of sinewy youth and ripe manhood tightly packaged, scantily clad in a Speedo-type swimsuit, a rarity in Yuba City then, when showing too much skin was considered immodest. Bobby was an exception to this and almost every other rule.

He charged the air with a palpable sense of excitement, like a sudden shift in wind direction. You could feel it, but you couldn't see it. That was my reaction, anyway. He did that to me.

Striding the length of the pool, he had to pass the lifeguard station with the coach sitting up on his tower. What Bobby did next was enough of a surprise that it caught my attention—and the attention of a few others. As he walked by the coach, he took the towel he had tucked under his arm and laid it down, still rolled up, at the foot of the ladder, deliberately, as if making some kind of statement or marking territory. Maybe it meant something; maybe it didn't. But he had definitely broken an unwritten rule. No one approached the coach or encroached on his immediate area while he was on duty. His space was his space and *he* approached *you*—mainly for discipline—"Don't run on the wet cement!" or "No cannonballing!" after a series of loud blasts on his whistle.

But Bobby had a talent for making up his own rules as he went along. He laid the towel down right there on the cement, as if the spot had his name on it, and strolled to the end of the pool, ignoring the attention he was generating. The Rose Marie Reids had, in the meantime, lifted to a prone position propped up on their elbows. The Brylcreem boys took notice. The entire fleet of poolside sunglasses turned and followed him to the diving boards. The surfaces of the coach's glasses, those mirrored kind highway patrolmen wore, followed too. A baseball cap shadowed his face, the only thing visible being the aquiline nose that gleamed white with zinc oxide. But interest registered loud in his body language, as he sat up from a slouched position in his canvas chair, redirecting his attention from the pool of bobbing heads and flailing arms to the figure in the red suit ambling by. A Greek chorus of Ray-Bans duplicated tiny, multiple images of him on their shiny surfaces, all turning in unison. A startling ray of sun struck them like a reporter's flashbulb, and every forearm raised up over the eyes to shadow the glare but not miss a second of this orchestrated presentation.

Bobby grinned to himself. He knew what he was doing. He was good at ignoring the attention he created and playing to it at the same time, his walk smacking of more self-satisfaction than usual.

He stood at the edge of the pool with his arms crossed over his chest and passed a toe back and forth through the water. For reasons I didn't understand but that did make me think, his gaze suddenly cut to the coach and I could have sworn they connected in some way, although the coach's sunglasses obscured his reaction. It seemed that their eyes rested, one on the other, in some kind of delay but only for a split second, with some degree of intensity that passed a silent telegraphy between them. Something was understood or acknowledged.

Did they know one another from before? Even though it was just a feeling, a kid's intuitions can be perceptive and vague at the same time. I paddled over to the steps to watch. By the time I was situated, Bobby had started climbing to the intimidating, frightening high board.

The coach, realizing what was about to happen, instinctively moved to clear that end of the pool. Waving his arms and blowing his whistle, he jumped quickly to his feet.

"Move to the sides! Move over! Get outta the way!" he shouted, pointing up to the high dive. Obediently, mechanically, like in a school fire drill, swimmers responded, crowding quickly to the edges or climbing out of the water. All eyes turned upward. A dive from the high board was an event. With Robert Reeves, Jr. executing it, it was a major event.

A quiet fell over the crowd. The peripheral noise around the pool diminished. The splashing water stilled. Feeling drawn into the expectancy in the air but also divorced from it, I found I was having a reaction I hadn't expected, physical, intense, and surprising. I did not know why it had happened, nor was I disturbed by it, but it raised questions by virtue of where I was at the time. Bobby's appearance in red and his strutting by, turning heads, the curious, almost electrical second between him and the coach, either real or imagined, started a quiet ringing in my ears. The sounds of cars crossing the bridge, their revving engines, were like intermittent drum roles or a pulse pumping blood through my veins at irregular intervals. The rapid sensations, one on top of the other, caused my body to react in a strange way. As I sat squatting in the shallow water, the stiffness of an erection pressed against the cold of my wet bathing suit. Was it a two-plus-two-equals-four equation? Possibly. But if it was, I had no comprehension of the implications.

Bobby stepped forward to the edge of the platform and looked down at the water, shifting his weight from foot to foot like an antsy colt, curling and uncurling his toes independent of each other as they searched for an edge to hold onto. He collected his body, his thoughts, calculated and militarily precise: feet together, legs straight, arms at his sides. His toes gripped the edge of the board like tensed fingers.

Seeing him standing there so high in the air, alone in concentration and thought, gathering energy, changed the reality of time for me, its tempo, how I experienced it. Anticipation dizzied me like a potent aphrodisiac.

The figure leapt into the air and *click*. My mind translated the human form as soon as it left the board, flying then sailing, free from the physical laws of objects in space. It was Icarus rising, suspended by a force that lifted and supported an exquisitely arched shape, linear and avian, rising higher and higher, crossing in front of the sun, bone white and blazing down, blackening the image in total eclipse, obscuring all detail and leaving the dark outline undiscernible. Somewhere within the seamless sky, the air gasped, caught its breath, gathering into it the suspended time. Falling was flying. For a little while. Below, everybody watched, stunned and reverent. Automatically, my brain recorded the images in slow motion with its cerebral camera . . . *click* . . . every detail—the curves, the shadows, every flexing part synchronized into every other part so I could replay it over and over like a note of music, the echoes of which resonate long after the initial note ends. *Click.*

At its zenith, the airlifted figure arched as if thrusting, mounting, then climaxing in ecstasy, and turned downward, became an arrow ripping through space, speeding toward the water and slicing the surface, barely disturbing it with a quiet, exact incision. On the sidelines, the audience held their breath. Waited. Then suddenly, Bobby, reclaiming human form, shot straight up out of the water like Neptune jettisoned from the sea and in three powerful strokes reached the edge of the pool, following with continuous, interlocking movements that propelled him effortlessly out of the water. With both arms pushing down on the edge, he secured a footing—one foot then the other—and stood upright, water beading on his body, trickling down his limbs and puddling at his feet. The erection pulsed against my bathing suit.

Applause broke the silence like a crash. Whistling. Catcalling. Bobby, with customary nonchalance, shook his head vigorously side to side several times, sending sprinkler-like circles onto hot cement in steamy circumferences, never acknowledging the crowd or the rush of admiration he had created. He walked to the low diving board, sat down, and leaned forward, resting his forearms on his thighs, looking down at the concrete as if he was the only person at the pool.

The applause faded and soon the mood and the activity around and the pool returned to a normal state of manageable chaos. *Screeeet!*

Screeeet! Two hits sounded from the whistle, the coach's green light. The melee of screaming children began to rise to its previous level and the Rose Marie Reids lowered themselves back onto their towels and back into themselves. The teenage boys, somewhat intimidated by the show-stopping performance of another male, the competition, sulked around rather than strutted, muttering to each other, clearly jealous at having had their thunder stolen.

The coach, however, did not settle back into his chair in the usual slouched posture. Sitting on the edge of the seat, he seemed agitated, unsettled, fidgeting, biting at a fingernail, looking as if he was debating himself. Then, scurrying down the ladder with the agility of a lizard, in quick short steps incongruous to his overall masculine demeanor, he went, with no mistaken intention as to where, directly to Bobby's side, planting himself on the board next to him, close, and aping Bobby's sitting position with his knees bent, legs apart, and forearms resting on his thighs, as though it was the posture that confirmed an established familiarity between them. Was that a fact or wasn't it? Or was it only an insinuation, a projection, a desire, maybe, coming from the coach?

The dialogue between them was too far away for me to hear, but from the expressions on both the faces and their body language, the brevity of the exchange, and from having been in a few similar situations in my adult life where seduction was at play, I imagine it went something like this:

"That was really some performance, kid."

"Uh . . . thanks," was Bobby's response, mechanical and distant. He stared straight ahead, not turning to make eye contact. He tilted his head, tapping it hard with the butt of his palm, jarring water out of one ear. I interpreted the behavior as guarded, an attempt to remain at a distance, despite his close proximity to the coach.

"You're some athlete." This elicited no response. "New around here, aren't ya?" Still nothing. "I sure could make swell use of you, er, on the football team, I mean. I'll bet you'd make a heck of a quarterback. Or a wide receiver, maybe?"

A look of icy detachment, or possibly repulsion, registered on Bobby's face. This part I have to imagine on my own. I was too far away to be sure. But he turned his head to the coach for the first time, looked him directly in the eye, and curled his lips into a smile that smacked of contempt, a smile that wasn't a smile at all, much like his father's, and said, "Dunno. Never played much ball."

With this last sentence he looked over the crowd and noticed a few people here and there watching the exchange with more than a passing interest. He seemed to recognize what that curiosity might mean and realized other people might also know a hustle when they saw one, some people having a nose for that kind of thing, the kind that makes for gossip. Not the good kind. Clearly uncomfortable with the sideline interest, Bobby squirmed, shifting back and forth from one cheek to the other.

"Nope," the coach continued, oblivious to Bobby's discomfort at the tone and implications of his comments. He was inordinately intense and driven by something that made him bolder than he might otherwise have been. Then, because he was either frustrated or stupid, he did something rash. He draped an arm over Bobby's shoulder like a close friend would do without thinking twice. It was the reckless move of a desperate hard sell—one that clearly, even from as far away as I was, made Bobby more edgy and more tense.

But the coach continued, still frustrated or stupid. "Not takin' no for an answer, buddy. Trust me. I can smell talent like yours a mile away. You're a natural."

"Maybe. I dunno. I'll think about it. But I gotta go now." Bobby slipped out from under the coach's arm and headed for the lockers. It was only then that the coach seemed to come to his senses, looked around, noticed the lingering stares, and went in quick little steps back to his perch.

Mom and I sat around in the sun long enough to dry off, drained of energy in the way overexposure in the direct sun dries and depletes. What had happened and what I made out of it stayed with me, still not quite sure of what I'd seen and felt, especially in light of my erection, which by then had disappeared. She said calmly, "Time to go. I need a few things from the store before I start dinner." *What had my mother thought of that spectacle?* I wonder now. *Mothers always know more than they let on. Or had I made something that was something it wasn't?* We left.

News traveled fast in Yuba City. When we pulled into our driveway and while Mom was taking the groceries into the house, I walked back to where Mrs. Hurlbert was working yet again in her rose garden on the other side of the fence. The rush of the swimming pool experience lingered in me, and I wanted to enthuse to someone about what I'd seen, even if it had to be her. So I did a quick rehash of the swan dive, minus the incident with the coach.

But in a small town nothing stays secret very long. In a sweat and bent over pulling weeds, she harrumphed like a sore loser, "Already heard about that. Vadna [another neighbor] takes the boys swimmin' there on Saturdays. That was a performance all right! Forget the dive.

Ask me, that coach's a little too interested in that kid. Maybe the kid, the coach, if you know what I mean!" I didn't, but that sounded a lot like a can of worms that begged to be opened and I wasn't about to be the one to do it. Not with her.

Besides, the day was winding down. Better things were happening. Sunset had been pure gold. Dusk was right around the corner. The mosquito jeep would be coming.

My mother was fixing dinner. I stayed outside to play, as the rest of the neighborhood kids did at that hour in the summer. The mosquitoes, fully squadroned that time of day, winged out in unstructured patterns and swarmed from the dark undersides of leaves and other hiding places. I joined the other kids, running in the street through the exotic blue-gray plumes of pesticide as the slow-moving county jeep crept down Brown Avenue. *Pssssssssssss. Pssssssssssss.* Rolling clouds hissed from the tanks on the tailgate and drifted in and around the houses on both sides of the street, wafting and settling like dry ice on a stage. When I heard "Dinner's ready!" coming from the back door of our house, I raced home, hungry and sweaty and smelling of DDT.

As the fall term approached and faculty meetings at the high school began, Coach Rice was all confidence to his colleagues—cocky, in fact. "Got this Reeves kid in my back pocket," he said. The department was ready and eagerly waiting. However, when the fall term started, the high hopes of the coach and the PE department were not to be. Bobby joined no team. Apart from daily stellar performances of all kinds in gym classes, he eschewed any kind of competitive activity at school, and the school's dream of a high school golden boy fizzled. Every day he left school on his bike and wherever he went, he went alone. This information filtered back to me bit by bit through an aunt of mine who had a friend who had a friend who worked in the office at the school. People talked.

Long after the day at the pool was forgotten by everyone, the experience stayed with me, as did the members of Reeves family themselves. And for years on clear winter days when the river was high, aching to reach flood stage, I would cross the bridge and out of habit glance down over the side, seeing nothing of the pool but the high dive platform, the flat four-by-eight-foot rectangle tiptoeing just above the water with its backside firm and stubborn against the fast-moving current, creating a berm, bubbling and foaming, as the water rushed around it. The melodrama of the swimming pool incident resurfaced in my melodramatic mind, and I let myself be swept back to the entanglement with Bobby and the secrets inherent in what was my passive, if eager, participation. It was often the cause of what my hand did under the blankets at night.

I loved reliving the past and the unthinkable things we'd done and wondered if I would ever experience anything like that again, sure that no one else could possibly feel the way I felt. Our history, Bobby's and mine, molded my behavior in many ways for a long time. I thought back on that particular Saturday many times. And wondered. Perhaps I had simply been witnessed to a really good swan dive. There may have been no connection to Bobby, the coach, and what happened after that. But I'd never know.

CHAPTER 3

A DATE
WITH SUPERMAN

I T WAS NINE O'CLOCK WHEN I WOKE UP that morning, that
anticipated morning, that anxiety-ridden morning, when I was
to appear at Bobby's front door. Two hours to wait. Two hours
during which I would worry and stew and work up a sweat. The
voices in my head, the what-ifs, had kept me awake most of the night.
A solitary mosquito jabbed at my ears and eyes and neck, buzzing,
buzzing, buzzing for hours, but even that was not close to the noise
in my head. I got up more times than I could count, turned on the
light, and, when my eyes had adjusted, took a rolled-up comic book
and stalked it, swatted it, thought I'd killed it. It kept coming back,
just like the voices did.

Sleep managed to slip in, unsettled and restless. The night never
cooled off, stifling, oppressively hot. I bolted up in bed still half inhabiting my scattered dream, my mind grabbing at fragments already
pulling away, trying to be forgotten, and lay drenched in a dark,
wrinkled blot on soaked sheets that had been crisp and white when
I had crawled to bed.

I lay on my back watching a fly crawl across the ceiling, moving
in fits and starts. I put myself in its place, trying to imagine what

it would be like to walk upside down in the world. The small black insect, scurrying aimlessly this way and that, reminded me of the coach coming down the ladder and hurrying over to Bobby. The thought switched to Bobby, the tight red bathing suit and his body arched high in the air above me. A connection between him and the coach and what went on between them after that was there somewhere, but I couldn't make heads or tails of it.

I got up, rubbed my eyes, stretched hard and high, and went to the mirror above the dresser. What I saw was what I expected to see every morning—sleep in the corners of my eyes and a cowlick, as vertical as a flagpole, at the back of my head. I leaned into the glass to pick the sleep out of my eyes, and a warning from my maternal grandmother, Nannie, suddenly came to mind, as if she were lurking somewhere in the mirror watching me: *Be careful what you ask for,* she seemed to say.

As quickly as it had come, the thought was gone, pushed right out of my head, as thoughts often were. Still, Nannie was right a lot of the time. On some level, what I heard her say from the mirror made sense. Having given herself completely over to God like a generous donation, her motives were good and true and in everyone's best interest. But today was not the day to think about that. And I didn't really understand what she meant anyway.

My chest felt as tight as a trussed chicken ready for a hot oven as I worried ceaselessly about any number of faux pas I was bound to make once I was at Bobby's place. How should I act? What was I going to say? Would he like me?

I avoided my mother, who was moving around in the kitchen. I didn't want to face her questions about my plans for the day and decided to pass the time hunkered down in my room, ending up doing things I'd already done. I rearranged my obsessively organized toy box, straightened the clothes already hanging perfectly straight in the closet, (my father had lowered the rod to accommodate my height), dusted the furniture I'd dusted the day before, and checked every drawer to make sure all things were properly folded. The warm air from the open window would dry the sheets and I would make the bed before I left, a habit I was equally obsessive about.

What to wear? After a considerable deliberation I ended up looking the same as I always did: tan short pants, red T-shirt, and tennis shoes. The shirt, was a mistake, a gigantic one, my first faux pas. Red was a good color for me, I'd been told. But it was not a good color for someone with a perspiration issue. I hadn't thought of this until I was crossing the street and half-moons were darkening my armpits.

———

I heard my mother run her bathwater behind the closed bathroom door. This was the time to leave. I quickly ate a bowl of Cheerios and milk and, as I left, I yelled down the hall, "Goin' to the park, Mom," confident no questions would come from this when I got back. I went to the park often. She wouldn't be worried. The screen door banged behind me as I jumped from the porch stoop directly onto the driveway, ignoring the two steps in between.

My exchange with Mrs. Hurlbert at the end of the driveway had been cut short by my cavalier use of "hell" as if it were a part of my everyday vocabulary. She *harrumphed* herself back to bending over in her Bermuda grass, mumbling about "young people these days," with her back to me and her butt in the air. I hurried across the street, which was empty of cars and people, certain I had arrived at the Reeves house undetected and under the cloak of secrecy where I had kept the invitation tightly shrouded. I rang the bell, and Bobby ushered me through the door before the chimes ended.

And there he stood—naked but for his droopy white socks. We faced each other for a long time. Or for what seemed like a long time, since time was standing still—as still as we were. The warm crescents in my armpits warmed and widened. "Now what?" I said to myself. Bobby shifted from one foot to the other, watching me watching him. I did the same. Sweat beaded on my upper lip and a thin stream trickled down my back. Bobby was sweating, too, a little, but unlike me, it worked in his favor, like everything else he did. His creamy skin gave off a luxurious glow, like a length of fine white satin. I was a wet, clammy mess.

The details of his body remain, as vivid to me now as they were then. The distance of years between then and now has had no effect on remembering, and a lifetime of words affords the adjectives and similes to describe him with more accuracy. I stood transfixed, the image galvanized in my brain and into my future.

The marble chest and torso had only the tiny interruption of nipples, hard and pink. From the broad shoulders and sinewy arms, the upper body tapered classically into stomach muscles that led to the apex of tight, curly hair entangled like fine auburn wire into a neat arch over a manhood that pulsed ever so slightly as I stared at it, seeming to be aware of my curiosity and responding with a curiosity of its own. His legs shifted and flexed from one to the other.

"Wanna see the house?" he said, breaking our stalemate.

"I guess," I replied sheepishly. What else could I say?

"C'mon. My room's in the back," he said. "But I want to show you something first."

His stockinged feet made padded thumps on the hardwood floors, giving cadence to pauses in his comments about this and that, none of which I can recall. But I noticed something unusual in his voice. A nervous tremor had found a place there, slight and cool but distinct. The house tour was one thing. What was going on in his head was another.

His butt muscles flexed, tightening and relaxing, the hamstrings in the back of his stringy but superbly developed runner's legs pulling taut in the long open stride. I was trying to keep up with him and to listen but couldn't help wondering how in the world, with no clothes on, he could be so nonchalant. It was a complete and total embarrassment for anyone in my house to be seen, accidentally or otherwise, in their underwear. Caution, or rather I should say great pains, were taken to see that this unspeakable event never happened. Did the entire Reeves family walk around the house like this?

Something else occurs to me now that occurred to me then. It registered while the details of his physique were imprinting themselves in my head and was almost as startling. It was a smell—a slight stinging one that reminded me of—what? I couldn't say for sure. Something vaguely antiseptic, like the room in the Rideout Hospital where I had my tonsils out. It was not at all like any of the familiar smells of familiar places, all of which instantly defined the place itself: Grandma Souza's kitchen that always smelled of something on the stove—garlic, onions, cumin, and bay; the Chinese restaurant in Marysville of fried rice and soy; the Nazarene church of musty hymn books (as my other sensibility perceived platitudes and hypocrisy, but that came later).

The Reeves house didn't smell like anything I'd smelled before and was like an additional presence—an atmosphere of particular density.

Everything in the house was beige or a version of beige with two notable exceptions that I glanced at in passing: a small pile of bright yellow *National Geographic* magazines stacked neatly on a table beside a tan, tweedy upholstered chair and a stiff, uncomfortable-looking sofa; and a green and yellow lazy Susan on the bare dining room table. I tried to visualize the family using it but somehow couldn't picture Bobby asking his father to please spin the mayonnaise.

I followed him into a bedroom that was clearly not his, evident in the stealthy way he entered, tiptoeing. So I tiptoed as well. We probably shouldn't have been in there. He led me to the dresser and opened the top drawer, which was just about at eye level for me. From what I could see, the contents were like those in my mother's dresser—soft, loose piles of pastel undergarments made of silky, slippery material with delicate lace-like trim in colors of blue, pink, and cream.

But Bobby reached to the back and brought out something I'd never seen before. It was hidden in there and out of character with the silky undergarments.

"He'll never miss it," Bobby said, tearing open a small square packet and pulled out what was inside. It was round, about the size of a quarter, and paper-thin, like a balloon, only more so, skin color, or trying to be skin color.

"Feel this," he whispered after he'd put it in my hand. It felt somewhat like skin, but not really. It was rolled up and flat, like some kind of travel-packed balloon to be blown up at the proper time. "He rolls one of these down on his this," Bobby said, pointing to his dick, which was noticeably less flaccid and pulsed when I looked at it, seeming alive somehow, "before he climbs on and sticks it in. You know. His pecker. Rolls it on like a glove."

I had no idea what he was talking about, but nodded, as if I did.

"C'mon," he said, taking it from my hand. I followed him out of the room, down the hall and into his bedroom. The door shut behind us with a sucking of wind and a contracting of space more than a noise. He leaned against it with both hands holding the doorknob at the small of his back, as *femme fatales* close doors in movies. He stood watching me for a minute, scratching the crown of one socked foot with the curled toe of the other.

The air was close, warm and thin, the din of the water cooler on the roof offering the only sound, a low, far-off rumble. I could almost feel the red vein of the thermometer hanging on the outside wall inching up. It was going to be a hundred-degree day. The direct rays of the sun were blocked from the room, held at bay by the pull-down window shade, but the force of the heat hammered at the glass, intruding to bathe the room and us in a defiant but softening glow. The heat would come through later.

Bobby's bedroom was like a movie set specially designed for actors and the specific parts they would play. It was a performance I would comfortably and willingly settle into in the weeks ahead when I returned a second time, a third time, and more. But as familiar as I was to become with the room, the perspective—the feeling of space and the atmosphere it projected—always struck me as if I were seeing it for the first time. Mountains on the wallpaper wrapped the room in desert and sky. Covered wagons drawn in a circle fortressed a handful of cowboys squatting around a slow-burning campfire showing no interest in our presence except for one burly, bearded fellow, who looked suspicious by nature and gazed surreptitiously at us from the corner of one eye while the others stared at the fire and poked the coals with a stick or drank coffee from dented tin cups. They appeared to be spinning tall tales to one another, cigarettes curling fine gray ribbons of smoke in the air while hanging from the corners of their mouths. Outcroppings of cactus, large and small, dotted the outlying desert like prickly Pillsbury Doughboys, and clouds, unevenly distributed, floated statically in random patterns, repeating themselves as wallpaper does. One far-away buzzard drifted on static thermals. The sand stopped abruptly where the walls met the shiny hardwood floors.

A brown braided throw rug lay between twin beds. There was a single-drawer nightstand in between them on which sat a ceramic lamp of a bucking bronco and rider waving one arm in the air and clutching the saddle horn with the other. The furniture was painted with coordinating Western-type motifs: cactus, lariats, and tumbleweeds. A Monterey-style dresser was on one wall. Each bed was shoved against their adjacent wall in such a way that put the suspicious cowboy intimidatingly close to whomever lay on the bed. Even though my house was just across the street, this room was another country.

As in the rest of the house, the colors were brown or beige. I think of the house now as an exercise in controlled neutrality, symptomatic of a pattern that extended beyond the décor, perhaps a statement that nothing in the Reeveses' world was left to chance and everything was always under control, as the house itself was.

In some way, the room was not unlike my own. It was obsessively neat and clean. There were no piles of dirty clothes. No plate of half-eaten food from a late-night snack laying around. No empty Coke bottles or candy wrappers anywhere. The closet door was half open and offered a glimpse at order consistent with everything else—the hangers were equally spaced, the clothes color-coordinated, and the shoes in precise pairs on the floor. For some reason, the similarity of this room to mine put me at ease. Bobby and I were alike, if only in this one superficial way.

What I was expecting to see I didn't see. There was no sign of athletic activity. No balls, no bats, no other teenage boy stuff. No dartboard, baseball cap, pet hamster cage or fish tank, bottles of dead bugs or cork boards with butterflies stuck in rows with straight pins-nothing to suggest Bobby was who he was. It was as if his physical presence alone answered that question.

My eye stopped at the bedspreads, optically dizzying if you looked too long, like opening your eyes after spinning around and around in place with them closed. In the center was a striking Palomino horse head staring at me with hard, black eyes, around which wavy patterns of evenly distributed tufts of chenille swirled and spilled over the edges of the beds. I tried to imagine crawling in under such an ominous creature and trying to sleep. I couldn't.

At this point I had become fairly relaxed with where I was, moderately comfortable even, despite the strangeness of Bobby's naked body, something I could have reached out and touched. He had proven to be, after all my apprehensions, engaging and attentive, playfully tousling my hair and giving my side a tickle, distracting me and forcing me to the giggles. Still, there was the underlying feeling that something wasn't quite right, a caution one of my voices whispered in the background. But what was "quite right" exactly? It was like I was in the middle of a complex puzzle with pieces that didn't fit but were in some way all leading to a bigger, more complete picture.

I thought of his father's comment: "Bobby tells me he'd like to have you. Over to the house, I mean." Then the drama at the swimming pool, the stares and the whispers. And now Bobby naked within a reach of my arm. Was any of this not quite right? And, if so, what was not right about it?

Bobby jumped onto one bed, standing over me taller than ever, again in the classic Superman pose with his hands on his hips, which then put his privates boldly and very near, very nearly, in my face.

"Faster than a speeding bullet," he said. "More powerful than a locomotive! Able to leap tall buildings in a single bound! Look! Up in the sky! It's a bird! It's a plane! No, it's Superman!" Just like the Saturday matinee serials.

The filtered light of the sun through the shade bathed him in a warm glow. He was all sheen, the moisture on his skin a conductor of luminosity. I thought, *Yes, you could be Superman*. (Ironically, the actor's name who played Superman on the screen was Reeves— George Reeves.)

Jumping back to the floor, Bobby steered me with his hands on my shoulders onto the bed, onto my stomach, and into the position we would be in to look at the comic book. Or so I thought. He lay down next to me and pressed the full length of his side against mine, sending the heat of his body through my clothes. The feeling was familiar and I relaxed, closed my eyes, and was, for a moment, taken back to those balmy nights my father carried me half-asleep from the State Theater to the car, my head nestled into the crook of his neck, the deep vibration of his voice to my mother a soothing, reassuring vibration.

But instead of putting the comic book in front of us on the bed, he turned my body to face his, draped his arm over my shoulder, and stared in my eyes, and it seemed like I was looking at a different version of the boy I'd seen before. Less charming. More aggressive. Intent and possessed by an idea or something else. He ran his fingers through my hair, over and over, stroking it, then down my back. His hand rubbed my ass for a while then his fingers pressed through the thickness of my pants and massaged my tight anus, gently at first and then harder in such a way that stimulated me and made me hard like I had been in the swimming pool. He pressed his front side and his curved stiffness against me. And then my voices joined in. There was a battle

Not there. Not down there.

Ummmm.

You should stop him. Should I? Yes. Do I want to? I don't . . . think . . . so. What should I do now?

His hand worked my belt loose, unbuttoned the top of my pants, and he slipped his fingers down the front, cupping my moist genitals in his palm. I shifted away. He stopped and removed his hand. There was something wrong about what he was doing, I thought, but I was confused about to how to react. My body said one thing. My head another. Something else—my heart?—still another. I was more stimulated than afraid, curious with lingering resistance. His hand on my hard penis had done nothing to put me off. And when his hand slipped back down my pants again, it was as if it had a right to be there and was determined this time to stay. I shifted away once more, but his hand stayed on me. The wall stopped me, pinning me between Bobby and the cowboy with suspicious eyes, still stoic and motionless and staring. He flipped me onto my back as easily as if I'd been a fifty-cent piece. The voices argued in all directions. Warnings. Threats. Encouragements. What-ifs. I lay on top of the horse head and heard the muted sound—metal on metal—of my zipper opening.

Bobby's breath was labored, panting. He wrangled my pants to my ankles quickly and with a skill that would only have been acquired through practice. And I lay exposed, naked. I lifted my head and saw his engorged penis, the protruding veins running vertically up and down the sides. I wanted to get away. I was afraid. I wanted to stay. It was as if I were giving myself up to an outgoing tide or strong current, carried along in the direction some part of me had intended all along. The strange and new excitement pumping through me was a force unlike any I'd known. Fear pulled one way and a compelling desire pulled another. I lay my head back down on the pillow. "Where's the comic book?" I asked in a faltering voice, not knowing what else to say. I had to say something.

"We don't need that now," he replied. "I'll show you how to fly anyway."

I stared at the cottony clouds dotting the ceiling as he took me in his mouth, warm and wet, sealing his lips around my penis and wetting it with saliva. He snailed up and down my small erection and low moans rumbled in his throat—garbled sounds—"ummm." I lifted my head just enough to watch his auburn hair flopping this way and that. The sensation, so new, one I'd never felt before, built and built as Bobby's skill in what he was doing tested and teased, his mouth slithering up and down, sometimes fast, sometimes pausing, varying the tempo, as if he was playing an instrument. I quivered, squirmed, was frozen in a stimulation impossible to fight. *Stronger than! Faster than!* The feeling, a dis-ease of the most exquisite kind, rose to a crest somewhere in my loins and exploded into shooting stars and colored lights. Far too young for ejaculation, there was, nevertheless, a peak and release so intense it shattered any other sensation I'd ever had. My body jerked, once, twice, three times in convulsive spasms, contorting me into a hard backbend arch. I collapsed on the bed, feigning to pull away even though I didn't want to, my wrists pinned down on either side. Bobby held me in his mouth until I was completely motionless, flaccid, satisfied, and empty of all energy in a voided space I'd never known.

He took a Kleenex from the drawer of the nightstand and wiped off what he had deposited on my leg, then tossed the tissue on the floor. The desert, the distant mountains, the paralyzed clouds all came back into focus. The cowboys had no reaction. Nothing had changed. Except everything had changed. We fell asleep side by side with his arm over my chest.

The sun was on the other side of the house when we woke up. Stifling heat had lagged behind the sun and had accumulated in the room. The desert reasserted its presence. The cowboys, in their circle, hadn't reacted to what had gone on, unfazed by what they'd been privy to.

Bobby sat up on the edge of the bed and leaned forward with his forearms resting on his knees as he had on the diving board. He acted as oblivious to my being there as he had been to the onlookers at the pool, unconcerned that I was beside him with my genitals exposed and my pants gathered at my ankles. I jimmied them up feeling—what? Redundant? Abandoned? Alone? I couldn't tell. The seconds of silence, the ones that felt like minutes, echoed the silence of my arrival but had changed in the way that silences can. It was louder now, having grown up, screaming with something lost and something found, a new awareness inhabiting it.

"I guess you should head home," he said. He seemed all of a sudden self-conscious and, I detected, in a way ashamed, the grin on his face forced, not convincing.

"Yeah, I guess so," I replied with my head down, staring at the braided rug. He walked me back down the hall, his hand in the middle of my back, past the beige interior, past the simulation of an ordinary family, past the sanitized smell plus the smell of the dried cum on his stomach he had missed wiping off, the combination disinfectantly acrid.

I stepped into the sun, cloudless and free of birds, white as bleached bone, shining down hard and thick with guilt and ecstasy—the wrathful eye of God passing judgment. My eyes squeezed shut against it. I blinked and blinked again and then again, as a new baby would, opening its eyes, over and over, as if to check that the world was still there. I thought the ache below my sternum was guilt, but it was not that at all. I felt as though I had stumbled across a trove of knowledge, vast and mysterious. It was like a magnet, an addiction that would pull me back across the street like someone seeking nourishment and finding it in the desert. In the next weeks and months, I would enter Bobby's house in a way that seemed as familiar as entering my own. The drapes would always be drawn and his parents not there.

"See ya later, buddy," Bobby said.

"Okay," I replied, retracing the steps to my back door, wondering what to do next. I wore my socks to bed that night. I still wear them to bed.

———◆———

Bobby and I continued to meet for weeks, or maybe it was months. I can't remember. Our sexual activity was always of a pattern. But, finally, when nearly caught in the act—his parents came home unexpectedly—sex in his bedroom was at an end. It didn't mean we stopped. We moved the activity outside and into the vacant lot next to my house, meeting there after dinner when it was still light and warm. We trampled avenues to the middle in the waist high weeds, me from my backyard and him from the edge of the street, and stomped down a space that was completely flat and visible to other eyes from no angle at all—a prickly bed of various volunteer weeds left to their own device, sprouting in the spring, proliferating first and then dying in the summer.

Our relationship ended. It had to. *Can I even call it a relationship?* Not long before the Reeves family moved away, an incident took place that was as shocking as a Roman Polanski movie can be. It was a culmination of Bobby and me, whatever we were, as disturbing as it was sudden. The day was warm and sunny, a slow coming-into-fall day in Doc Fippin's field a block away from where we lived where two neighborhood friends my age and I had constructed a three-sided fort of hay bales that lay strewn over the large, dry open expanse of shorn alfalfa stretching from Gray Avenue to the county highway acres away to the west.

I can't remember the exact details. I can only liken the experience to a nightmare from which you bolt upright afterward, heart pounding. But as I said in the beginning, nothing is really like or as anything else, so comparisons are often way off. Bobby had suddenly appeared almost out of nowhere. We stood, surprised and at first pleased that he would take the time to grace us with his presence, still the neighborhood star and all. With no to-do, no groundwork, no conversation, no seduction, no finesse, one by one, starting with me, he had our pants down around our ankles and, one by one, starting with me, in succession, sucked us off. Rows of red-winged blackbirds spectated, fluttering their wings occasionally and commenting in bird language as they clutched their yellow claw-fingers to the phone lines running along Gray Avenue. Riders in sporadically passing cars turned their heads absentmindedly, noticing with no invested interest the small shoulder-sets of three upper torsos in the distance standing in a semi-circle behind bales of hay that offered no clue as to the outrageous demonstration of group hypnosis and mind-body control taking place down below.

Detaching itself from my body, my mind drifted above the macabre scenario, momentarily suspended in the sky like the swan dive, looking down at the three of us, dazed as deer in headlights, offering no resistance to the bizarre violations. And then it was over. And then he was done. And then he was gone. Just like that. Speechless, and staring blankly at one another, we pulled up our pants without speaking of what had just happened or what, if anything, to do about it. There was nothing *to* do. We walked home, not how we arrived as a threesome, but separated, each with a different, slowly paced stride. We never spoke of this afterward.

Before the end of the first school term, the Reeves moved away, leaving as inconspicuously as they had arrived. Unnoticed. They were here. And then they were gone.

CHAPTER 4

THE CAGE FULL
OF MONKEYS

MARGARET HUDGENS AND I were both nine years old when we were put together as dance partners at the College View Roller Palace. I had been hastily recruited from the "Busy B" class when we were paired for the juvenile dance competition at the California State and Pacific Coast Regional Roller-Skating Championship in San Diego only a few months away. At the time, a competition of this kind was a drudgery and an annoyance, and its significance to my future was not immediately apparent. But, although we fared badly—in other words, we lost—a competitive spirit was born in me, an addiction, really, that created a dedication to physical exercise on which the foundation of my overall health and emotional welfare was built over the course of a lifetime. Problems that seemed insurmountable, as well as several life crises, were tempered by a vigorous physical workout. Time at the gym became almost meditative.

The rush I experienced in the San Diego competition jolted my psyche and was, coincidentally, the precursor to a jarring event later that afternoon at the zoo, one that resulted in a personal epiphany of monumental significance.

Margaret was four inches taller and outweighed me by a good thirty pounds, although "good" is probably not the best way to describe the discrepancy. Along with other couples in our age group from various parts of the seven western states, we would execute our best versions of the Collegiate, the Schadash, and the Glide Waltz. Execute, the verb for execution—exactly what our performance felt like in the three and a half minutes of scrutiny by the panel of stone-faced judges. I was completely unqualified, having skated for less than a year. And even though I had been advanced from the first-level, beginner's "C" class to the second-tier Busy B rather quickly, my ability was hardly sufficient to qualify me for competition of any kind. But Margaret needed a partner, and her father, Kess, owned the skating rink.

Margaret was a middle child with all the baggage usually associated with being shoehorned into that unenviable position. She cried at the drop of a hat, an attention-getting device she used a lot during the lessons she and I crammed into those few months, both of us feeling the constant pressure of being corrected and corrected and corrected by our coach, Danny McNeice. He was one of the best in the country, recruited from Boston when the rink first opened. Kess had managed to lure him to Marysville, an unlikely place and a town way too small for a professional of Danny's caliber; he could have had his pick of any skating rink in the country. It had to have been the rink itself. It was the newest and biggest in California, a state-of-the-art facility at the time.

Danny had a high bar with regard to what he expected. Margaret and I were low-bar recruits. In trying our best to meet his standard and failing, Margaret cried and I sulked. As you would imagine, neither ploy of tears or moods improved our three dances.

The rink was in a residential area of East Marysville across the street from the Lucky market. Kess had named it the College View Roller Palace despite the fact it had no view of the college and was not even in the near vicinity inasmuch as the college was about ten miles on the other side of the Yuba River, as the crow flies. Why and how he came up with the name is a bit of history lost to time, much like how and why First Street in Yuba City disappeared or, in the pages of this story, what the true content of the conversation was between Coach Rice and Bobby that Saturday at the swimming pool.

Kess was determined that all of his three children be represented in San Diego—the first public showing for the Marysville/Yuba City skating team. His oldest daughter, Sonia, and his youngest, little Donna, had already been paired with better-trained boys—all height and weight appropriate. Margaret got what was available and could be scrounged up. That would be me. More Hudgens kids, future competitors, were on the way. They always were. In my years as a roller skater, I can't remember Ruby, Kess's wife, ever not being pregnant. If she was, this is nevertheless how I remember her, perhaps because of the provocative comment she often made: "One on and one in," she used to cackle, unapologetically breastfeeding the one "on" in the ticket office in full view of every customer coming through the doors. Shock. Amusement. Disgust. I saw all of the above at one time or other on faces that passed by her as they bought their ticket. It didn't matter to her. Ruby was Ruby.

Although I was totally not up to the competition part of the trip, I was excited about the promise of San Diego. It came also with the promise of seeing the world-famous San Diego Zoo when judging was over. The first phase of the competition was the "Eliminations" preceding the "Finals." Eliminated, Margaret and I would surely be, and I would be free to leave.

My primary goal was to see the monkey house. I had been infatuated with Tarzan and all the Tarzan films for years — Cheetah, human-like and tremendously appealing; Johnny Weissmuller, the Olympic swimming champion, who swung through the jungle in a brief leather loincloth on vines that were always in the right place at the right time. I could not have known that an "aha" moment was also waiting for me, one that would bring clarity and a revelation I couldn't have anticipated. I'm getting ahead of the story.

———————

In a new, black 1949 Chevy coupe, my parents and I joined the caravan of cars meeting in the parking lot of the skating rink, having made one stop at Jack Carlin's Men's Store on Plumas Street to pick up the rented tuxedo in which I was to perform. It was referred to as my "costume"—I loved costumes—and I was going to look smashing. My first tuxedo: white gabardine jacket, maroon bow tie and matching cummerbund, onyx shirt studs and cufflinks, and smart black trousers with thin black satin stripes down each leg. The whole deal. In the hubbub of getting ready, however, we had neglected to check the fit, which was a size too large, dramatically adding to the height/weight discrepancy between Margaret and me. My boney wrists and scrawny neck showed measurable air space between cuffs and wrists, neck and collar. Margaret's top and skirt were made of clingy white sateen that attached itself to her and the extra thirty pounds with a dedicated affection, making her appear just that much larger and me just that much smaller. Her Dutch Boy hairdo and my pompadour, neither of which compensated for the height difference, were spray-net stiff and pomade-rigid, respectively, completely immobile at rest and in motion.

It was July. The skating rink was big. And hot. The gigantic swamp coolers on the roof were doing what they could but were only moving the hot air around quickly, as if in a panic. Their overhead noise was a din, not quite a distraction, in the background to the Hammond organ, the standard instrument to accompany dance skating. Margaret and I waited on the sidelines, perspiring, most of the perspiration mine. A white square of canvas printed with the number 26 was pinned on my back. We were called. "Onto the floor, please, numbers 17, 26, and 59 for the Glide Waltz," the voice on the loudspeaker summoned. Showtime. My heart leapt into my throat. We took the floor and rolled into starting position.

There is something about your emotional state that has a direct bearing on the passage of time. In your head, the hands of the clock slow down or speed up depending on what you are anticipating—pleasure or dread. The minutes flew by as we waited to go onto the floor. But, once there in the throes of competition, the three and a half grueling minutes flew by like three and a half years, making the Glide Waltz feel more like the Boston Marathon. Even though this took place decades ago, I still cringe as I reconstruct the image of us and how we stood out from the others—for all the wrong reasons. Our ridiculous appearance. Our choppy performance. Awful.

When the end finally came, we left the floor winded and soaking wet to the sound of approving, if spotty, applause from our parents and the handful of College View teammates. Without going into detail about the following two dances, the Collegiate and the Schadash, you may assume they went as well as the Glide Waltz. You would be right.

1st Place, National Juvenile Dance, Cleveland, Ohio, 1950.

Nothing more on this need be said except that my skating career did ultimately take off and have a happier ending. And as I said, a fierce competitiveness had been born in me even with the thundering defeat. With a new partner the following year, Vicki Pitts, height and weight appropriate, success came. We skated to many notable wins. But for now, my job for the College View was done. I had served my purpose with valor. The Hudgens girls had their fifteen minutes of fame, if only in three and half minute increments. And it was time to move on. I changed out of the soaking wet tuxedo and back into street clothes, and we, my family and I, headed for the zoo.

We arrived a little before noon, feeding time for the monkeys. "You have to see it. Unbelievable," was what a neighbor lady had told my mother one day in the market. "Meet you at the flamingos in an hour," I said to Mom and Dad and started toward the monkey house, the location easily found on the map at the entrance.

"Okay, Richie. Be careful." This was the same caution I heard and would hear from my mother a million times from childhood through college, adulthood, the disco days of the 1970s and '80s, burning both ends of the night, cruising through dark places, the many men after midnight moving through my nights like passing comets, the slither of furtive sex, and the brief, white-hot efflorescence that burned out fast, liaisons that ended as they began—undramatically, suddenly, and without comment, the well-intended relationships with short sell-by dates, trouble in the guise of blue eyes and blue jeans, affairs that didn't last, the AIDS crisis and the aftermath. Sometimes I heeded her warning; sometimes I didn't. Sometimes I needed to go out, search for feelings, sometimes the absence of feelings. But here I am.

Stepping through the heavy commercial doors to the inside of the big building that housed the monkeys, I had an overwhelming feeling of déjà vu when the hydraulic rod slipped back into the cylinder attached to the top of the door as it slammed shut behind me with a loud KA-BANG-CLICK. I had never been there before. And yet . . .

There was a sense of great agitation. It started with increased chatter and built quickly as I approached the main area, which was filled with raucous monkey language. The first voice I heard was an attendant.

"Hey, Joe. Watch that big male! Don't let him get behind you!"

"He's just horny. I'm not worried."

"He bared his teeth! You'd better watch it!"

"Aw, he's got off already. Look at that female up top there. She's grinnin' ear to ear."

"Yeah, but check the rest of 'em. They've gone berserk!"

"It's that kid there that's just come in." He indicated me with a tilt of the head in my direction. "They're showin' off," he continued, "You know how they do. Them monkeys. They love an audience."

The floor-to-ceiling cage took up the whole of the huge interior space except for a perimeter walkway for visitors to circle the activity inside it, take pictures, and hand out peanuts, which all the signs said not to do. The heavy wire was painted black and almost disappeared, so you felt you were in the cage with the animals, a space that replicated a jungle as detailed and complete as if it were somewhere in Africa— running streams, full-sized palm and coconut trees, rubber plants as tall as houses and various pools of water surrounded by sand, rocks, small caves, and a huge network of platforms and swings.

The food had been put into natural stone-like receptacles or on the ground. The monkeys fed in groups or grabbed something and scurried off to eat alone, but all looked at me in unison when I had entered, my appearance having triggered a frenzy that turned into a deafening noise. Hairy arms and legs flew in every direction, almost in a blur.

The dominant males charged up to the wire, challenging me, screeching and howling at the top of their lungs. They clung to the bars and thrust their arms through, grabbing at me, or flew through the air from limb to limb as if possessed by demons. They catapulted from perch to wall to rope, from perch to wall to rope, over and over again in endless circles. One or two masturbated, staring at me with wild red eyes and glistening bared teeth. Timid females and small adolescents scurried to the safer recess of rocks or clutched each other, shivering and worried. A hand snatched a bit of food then devoured it as if it were the last on earth. This frenzy, this confusion, created its own curious agitation in me, but mental, not outwardly physical. I didn't know what it was or why I should react this way. One thing was clear—I had been the cause of the chaos. I was also the target.

All the hard surfaces magnified the noise, and it reverberated back and forth like a giant echo chamber, magnifying in my head, familiar and disturbing. And all at once, the walls started to close in. I was terrified. I felt like I was suffocating. *Get me out of here! I've got to get out of here!*

I raced from the building and rushed out into the glare, blinded by the sun. I got my bearings then collapsed on my knees on a small patch of grass. A recurring nightmare came back where I was struggling to move. I didn't know where or why. My feet were heavy, bogged down in thick dark mud. I strained to reach people standing somewhere in the distance, but as I got closer, they got smaller rather than larger and then they disappeared.

I had been in that cage before. That cage was in me. The chaos was not new. It had been inside me forever. What I had just witnessed was a replication in the flesh of what had been inside me for as long as I could remember. I had walked into and out of my own head.

CHAPTER 5

THE RITE OF SPRING: PART 1

ADOLESCENCE WAS A TIME OF TRANSITION, physically and emotionally, for boys and girls. Until then, friends were anyone of either sex you were inexplicably drawn to; "attraction" had little meaning other than "I like you." The division between the sexes was becoming distinct—females' breasts were no longer flat but swelling like spring buds while male hormones were more site-specific, above the belt and below—voices began to change, underarm and pubic hair appeared, male voices changed and, although not deep yet, resonated with the entitled timbre of young men. They still lived outside the realm of cynicism and irony, and neither sex had experienced the extreme pleasures of the flesh that I had. Nor the myriad of feelings that went with it. Of this I was fairly certain. Based on what? Nothing.

My attraction to both sexes was more or less equal, except for the intrusion of Bobby's memory and the reconstruction in my head of our sexual activities. Spontaneous erections came and went—daily, often several times a day—unpredictable and at inappropriate times. My mind seemed to have no control over my body. Nocturnal emissions. Whacking off under the sheets. Luxuriating in a warm bath, absent of energy and watching the jizz float and slide down the drain in soapy water. It was during this time that Jack came into my life, when love and expectation seemed to be my own personal discoveries and when lust and innocence were in a strange configuration with each other.

Johnathan Pierce Swift was a semi-feral twelve-year-old when we became friends, or almost friends, in the seventh grade. It was in those early days that I was caught by him, unaware of the final consequence. He was an odd and new brew with a manner that was as unsettling as his name was noble. He was called Jack, which lent itself to easy nicknames—Jack be nimble, Jack-of-all-trades, Jack-off. I found myself drawn to him as much for the inconsistencies I detected beneath his careless exterior as the sensitivity in himself he chose to ignore.

As potent a figure as he was in my youth, the connection we would ultimately share—physical and emotional—was almost at a remove and, as a result, I think of him and our time together from a distance that is as great as the accumulation of years that separates us now.

An initial delicacy formed between us that was little more than the curious impulses of two boys who observed each other, constrained by shyness and a lack of social confidence, and sustained by a pretense of indifference. But within the obvious curiosity, there was a need to communicate and, as a result, a sort of strained esteem emerged, taking our interaction to the level of feint and innuendo, which I inevitably expanded in my head and made more significant by my fertile imagination.

When we did talk, what did we talk about? I wish I could remember. Nothing of great importance, just like the surface of any boyhood interaction. When we shared an activity, what did we do? Nothing very memorable. But it all felt special in that way the young have of making something out of nothing. So we talked as brothers might, looking here and there, as we prattled about this or that, trying to think of things to say, unsure and too cautious to venture into feelings that wanted expression. At the same time, we were unable to ignore the buzz, the stirring attraction into which both of us were becoming innocently entangled. Awkwardness acted in reverse of what it might have, deepening rather than dispelling the mutual attraction.

In high school, we would eventually share a physical intimacy that was real, but one that registered on me, and perhaps on him, too, as unreal, something you might only dream. And as a result, my obsession for him, or rather, what I constructed in my head about the two of us, took on a life of its own and became something other than what it was, creating my fantasy of what the perfect relationship should be. It took shape as a notion, a goal, an ideal that would direct, as well as condemn, many other relationships. From my experience with Jack, I formed a personal ideology, a flawed philosophy about the perfect union of two people that lay in a liminal crease between fact and fiction—and was impossible to sustain.

I still don't fully understand what about him could have precipitated such a thing. He was scruffy, unkempt, like he'd just gotten out of bed. Trouble followed him around like the ragged strings on his pant leg. But somewhere within the dishevelment, there was a seam running through, something sleek, like a trout in water. His eloquent calf eyes, flashing from time to time with cool impertinence, could only be half appreciated beneath the lazy eyelids, but it never obscured the poetry I sensed within him. I found myself delicately at ease in his presence.

His jaw was disturbingly sculptural, acutely angled, holding his beauty in eerie balance within its own neglect. Unlike Bobby Reeves, Jack's charisma was born of indifference—neglect rather than concern—in and of itself an appealing contradiction. Like Bobby, he had the power to bore into and inhabit my thoughts, not so much because of what he said or did but what he withheld. He was somehow both sweet and monstrously dangerous and, like opium, easy to go along with.

We must have been in earlier grades together, but I don't remember that. However, the day I took notice of him, I remember clearly because it gave me a quick sense of calm, as if I recognized someone I had known before.

Rain during the night had left the playground wet and cold with blusters of wind. Roiling clouds had cleared the sky of birds. Classes were at midmorning recess, but the off and on showers kept any form of exercise at a minimum and only a brave few ventured out into the weather. There was one basketball fanatic making jump shots on the playground, and Jack was absentmindedly hitting a tetherball around the pole, his thoughts somewhere in the wind and drizzle. I had been watching from under the covered breezeway where most of the other kids congregated, huddled together in groups waiting for the bell. When it rang, he started back, and, as if by instinct, like a deer suddenly aware of being watched, turned his head toward me. Our eyes locked briefly in a subtle connection that was slightly unnerving and at the same time impossible to ignore.

"Do I know you?" he asked with an impish grin as he passed by, pausing only long enough for me to say with the slightest feather of flirtation, "I don't know. Do you?"

"I do now," he said, bumping my shoulder with his, familiar and teasing, as if we were already friends. He continued into the classroom, the grin still on his face, not looking back.

To the north beyond the rain and wind, the sky was cast-iron black. Nature's timpani of thunder, traveling in blue-black clouds, reverberated in the distance, moving like a vast state of mind with a force whose aim was to confound. By afternoon, great crashes of lighting electrified preternatural darkness, and sheets of heavy rain beat like whip lashes on the classroom windows. The storm was here.

After that first exchange, we associated infrequently, hardly even speaking for what seemed like a long time, the silence balanced on an edge with no indication of which way it would fall. Then for some reason, the ice broke like a spring thaw and we began interacting freely and more often. There was something about the way he looked at me in which I detected an understanding that lay deeper than facial expression, more like a secret code that was to evolve between us, like a backward glance held in a slight pause that felt like the first step in the subtle business of indicating desire.

We became better friends, but still in a way I can only describe as slender, the only common thread between us a vague melancholy that somehow managed to bridge the distance in a way neither understood. It lay in some secret place like the *saudade* tucked away in my Mediterranean genes.

One day, with boldness that was uncharacteristic, I walked up to him and said, "Wanna go to a movie?" I had no idea where this courage came from.

He paused for a second and looked down at his shoes. I thought I detected a grin, but I wasn't sure. "Saturday?" he replied, as if it had been his idea.

"Okay," I said, also with a pause, to credit him with the idea. "I'll meet you there." Fluttery inside but coyly nonchalant, I walked off. That was that.

We met at the State, a fading Spanish-Renaissance style theater from the glory days of cinema. It stood waiting, grandly, as it always did, when our parents dropped us off in front. We got our tickets from Mrs. "Battle-axe" Barnes, who stared at us from behind large, horn-rimmed glasses with a face like a pale Shar-Pei. We entered the elaborate lobby, symmetrically laid out with faux Corinthian pillars on either end anchoring the dual sweeping stairways leading to the loge. We crossed the worn Deco-Florentine-style carpet to the glass-fronted counter, bought popcorn and Cokes, and entered the main auditorium.

The movie was not crowded that day, and Jack and I had entire rows of seats to pick from. We sat somewhere in the middle as the Wurlitzer organ played familiar intermission tunes. The dimmed lights cast a patina on the faded, gilded glory of the vast interior, its history marked with generations of discarded chewing gum stuck to the bottom of the fold-up seats. The lights went down and the movie started. Jack, engrossed in the film, seemed indifferent to my presence, even as, from my slouched position, I let my leg swing into his every so often. In the light that flashed from the changing action up on the screen, I glanced over for a reaction. There was none.

After the movie, as we stood outside waiting for our rides, a tension had mounted in him, a palpable strain standing between us, and eye contact avoided. *I shouldn't have,* reliving my clumsy advances.

"Pretty good popcorn, huh?" I said breaking the silence. Still no comment. He had retreated to another place.

"I guess I'll see ya," I said, as we left in separate cars. And that was that. After a few chilly weeks of not speaking, my frustration forced a second bold move. I suggested another movie "date," as if it had been a regular thing with us. What did I have to lose? My desire to be with him in the dark had grown stronger than my fear of rejection.

"How about another Saturday movie?" I said, as if the chill had never been. He picked at his fingernail, frowned, didn't look up from whatever else he was doing, and said, "I'm working on the pickup with my dad Saturday." And that was that.

I'd fucked it up. I wasn't interesting enough, or cute enough, or clever enough, and emotional hand-wringing that our friendship was out of reach, too much to hope for, came with the fear. But then, from out of nowhere, his eyes flashed with renewed interest, inviting and resisting as well, and at that moment, without realizing it at the time, I had learned something about him that would complicate our future relationship. He was the stuff of desire *and* conflict. Much like myself.

As the days went on, sometimes we would find ourselves alone on the playground, distant and apart from everyone else. *Did he plan for us to meet this way?* I would wonder. *Given up something to be with me?* It felt like it. Ambiguous feelings not possible to explore began to take shape, ones that fostered thoughts of desire that were strung together like beads on a string, more elaborate and abstract than I'd had with Bobby, and all the more puzzling. Past images of Bobby mixed with present ones of Jack. I was trying to find an equation where there was none. Different and the same, they were both unknowable.

As strong as the intense and unyielding sexual pull had become, sex seemed not only unlikely but unreasonable. Because I had *had* sex with Bobby frequently, and because my pubescent sexual impulses were all over the map now, I couldn't help but project the past, Bobby's and mine, onto the present even though one thing was clear: what I wanted from Jack was not what I had wanted from Bobby. Not exactly. I just didn't know what it was. And as it turned out, it was not only different, but a lot more.

Thoughts of Bobby came and went constantly (and would for a long time). My voices, aggressive, persistent, pondered what I saw as a bleak sexual future. *When? Who with? Will it be like with Bobby?* It had been six years since the Reeveses had moved away, and Bobby and I had played out a relationship on a vastly different field than the one Jack and I were on. He was the pursuer. At first. And I was the pursued. Then, before long, I was a willing participant who encouraged, orchestrated when possible, sex with him. I wanted what he wanted.

What Jack wanted was a question mark, muddled in high school when, by our freshman year, his moods grew sometimes darker than I had seen, presenting as shadows in his expression, ones I hadn't noticed before, dark, but tender, like a bruise. At the same time, the turn of his mouth had grown more intimate, more magnetic, more sexual, day by day, year by year. I also discovered a conflict in him when we shared the same gym class—an acute paranoia about the large birthmark that ran along the left side of his torso, the existence of which would have him race back to the locker room ahead of the class so he could shower and be dressed and gone before they arrived. By accident, I caught a glimpse of it once when excused early from class for a doctor's appointment and had glanced over at the shower as I left the locker room. He didn't know I had seen him.

What part did this physical stamp play in the improbable and ultimately unfixable nature of our relationship? I wouldn't learn the answer. I'd only gain some insight. Later.

CHAPTER 6

THE RITE OF SPRING: PART 2

*L*ATER HAD BECOME A CATCHWORD when we were in seventh and eighth grades, and it followed us into high school. "Later," he'd say, drawing his hand across my waist as he walked by. Innocent enough when we were younger, but by high school, *Later* took on a different feel. It was in every touch, even if the word was unspoken. Sensuous now, it was covertly erotic as the same hand moved from my waist to a place higher on my back, resting there just long enough to send a signal. I wondered *Does he mean what I think he means?* I could never be sure. It there was a foot of space between us, I would do whatever I could to fill that distance; brush against him, perhaps—a hip, a shoulder, some part of me—to find the satisfaction I needed: touch.

If I grabbed his bicep and he resisted, he would flex the muscle, hardening it as if preening; the rigidity of his arm aroused me. Hard muscles had that effect. I clung to the word *Later*, picked over it, in it, and pulled from it what I wanted. *Does he mean, 'I'll see you later'? Or 'I wish, yearn, can hardly wait to see you later?'* Not knowing drove me crazy.

Sometimes we'd bump hips—"Watch it, doofus," he'd say—or playact that verged on violence. Light fisticuffs could get rough and annoying. But annoyance was part of the pleasure. *Later* could also be spoken in a quick meeting of the eyes.

I conflated the word into a secret code that spoke to a future rendez-vous, a promised mutual assignation. *Later* became as elastic and subtle as Jack himself.

During Easter vacation of our freshman year, *Later* played out over the course of a long Saturday night, one that stretched into the dawn of Easter Sunday morning. Jack and I and another friend, Ken Van Horn, planned to drive to the Easter Sunrise Service, an annual event held jointly by several churches at the uppermost point of the Sutter Buttes, a small mountain range about twenty miles west of town.

The plan was to stay up all night, drive there at dawn, and see what all the hoopla over Sunrise Service was about. For lack of anything else, it was something different to do—the best we could come up with—and proved to be an inspiration fated to crumble into nothing the next day after a night that was fated to crumble to nothing in the same way.

What had led up to this? It's hard to say. It was 1955. I was superficially aware of things happening in the world, but news of a national or global sort didn't hold any particular interest for me. Who cared what was going on in Alabama? The Salk vaccine had cured polio. Rosa Parks was arrested. But I was duly self-involved; anything outside of my immediate sphere was nothing to inspire much consideration. Rosa Parks? Who was that, anyway? And I didn't know anyone with polio.

My world revolved around the immediate, the personal, things that were full of sight and sound—movies, rock and roll, Elvis, Chuck

Berry, and the Platters, whose big hit, "The Great Pretender," I knew by heart. Wasn't I the great pretender? What new film was playing at the State? That was important. Who was going steady with whom? That was important. Had Feldman's Men's Store gotten any new colors of V-necked sweaters in? That was important.

The one exception was James Dean's death, sudden and violent. It hit me hard. It had meaning. His rise as a teenage icon had swept me up with the rest of my generation. Dean was sharing his aura of sexual fluidity with me personally. I could feel it. *He gets it,* I thought. *He would get me.* The violent end he met scared the hell out of me.

Birds Eye Frozen Fish Sticks were introduced into American kitchens to great success; Perez Prado's Latin-tempoed "Cherry Pink and Apple Blossom White" gave me a boner when that trumpet caressed and teased the sexy note, slid it tantalizingly up and down before picking the melody up again, arousing and tormenting like prolonged masturbation. Other subtleties provided physical stimulation, like dragonflies careening in locked pairs, one atop the other could mean only one thing. Flesh itself held the hot pulse of love. Everything bristled with intimacy in the intimacy of my small world, a place chock-full of forbidden thoughts and outré ideas. What lay ahead with Jack was chock-full of forbidden thoughts and things outré as well.

———

I had borrowed my dad's work car, available at night whenever I wanted it as long as it was back at a reasonable time. This time was an exception. The following day was Sunday and a holiday, and my parents approved my staying out. When I told them what we were going to do, they looked at each other as if to say, "Such a fine thing to do to celebrate Easter. What a good boy."

Exactly how that night materialized, I'm not sure. I might have orchestrated it. Or it may have been that peculiar kaleidoscope of circumstance that throws different elements together and rearranges them in an unexpected pattern. Or it might have been that I had access to a car at an age when nobody else I ran around with did. I'd like to think that wasn't it.

The three of us were in the front seat when I pulled into one of the inclined spaces at the Auto-See, the drive-in movie referred to as "the Passion Pit" or more graphically, "the Finger Bowl." I hooked the speaker on the car window and rolled it back up as much as possible, leaving only a small crack at the top. It was cold. The movies were reruns of what had been shown at the State months before. Didn't matter. We were just killing time.

We spread out in the front and back seats. Ken took the front and Jack and I jumped in the back and got under the blanket I'd had the presence of mind to bring. It was our only source of heat. Running the engine to run the heater was using gas we couldn't afford. It was under the blanket that *Later* started.

Our legs, Jack's and mine, were crossed, mine over his, his over mine, in a lackadaisical way. Physical contact with him, someone I'd been obsessing over for a long time, produced the inevitable—not unexpected but possibly problematic—hard-on. *Has he got one too?* I assumed so. Hoped so. Would have bet money on it. Even in cold weather, hard-ons had a way of happening.

We had no interest in the film—a grade-B production we'd seen before. A movie of my own was playing in my head. It had nothing to do with the one on the screen. Restless, we shifted around a lot. It was during a readjustment of body parts that Jack's forearm dragged across my crotch and across my boner. His arm, as if it had a mind of its own, paused there. I glanced over at him, the grin on his face telling me what he'd done, he'd done on purpose.

The voice in my head said, "Don't do anything! Nothing!"

Rumors had flown wildly around about Rad Dwyer at the baseball team's sleepover. His "accidental sleepwalking" after the lights went out and how he was discovered fumbling with the fly of teammate's pajamas flashed through my mind like a laser beam. "For fuck's sake! I walk in my sleep!" That was his excuse the next day and for days after that. No one bought it. I was afraid that similar rumors could spread about me. I had a suspicion that things like that were already being implied here and there. Guys who don't have cars are a jealous and vindictive lot. And at the rate rumors spread about something like this, I'd be finished. Fruity behavior, or even the insinuation of it, was a stigma impossible to get rid of.

The moment passed. Jack and I settled into a looser entanglement, still interlocked, after a fashion. Nothing was said, hinted at, or joked about. It was as if what happened never happened. Ken, sitting sideways in the front with his feet stretched out on the seat, had been watching the movie *and* us from the corner of one eye and sensed, I was sure, maybe with some kind of unspecified interest, something was going on in the back seat. Not much got past him. He had a nose. Fortunately, he wasn't a gossip. He was a friend who would never spread that kind of rumor about me.

We endured the movie to the end with little talk and no further incident. I was having a condensed conversation with myself, dissecting

Jack's every gesture, every glance, every tilt of his head, every twitch, for what it might mean. *What is he thinking? Was that really an accident? Was he trying to tell me something? Was it a first move? Testing the water? Should I reciprocate in some way? Fuck!*

My gut told me the promise that had been hovering over us since grammar school, the one the voices couldn't stop arguing about, the one that kept me awake nights, was on the verge of being made good. That's what I wanted to believe. *But how could I know?* In the meantime, the movie ended. We filed out in the line of other cars. My voices didn't stop. I knew they wouldn't. *Later* was getting closer.

———————

It was three o'clock in the morning, that hour so remote that it seems nowhere on the clock, that place where deep thoughts seep from the psyche and are, as someone said, "the three a.m. of the soul." It was the time of night when the hour itself doesn't make a difference; the time of night when the world is dead with sleep and the air has a sinful thrill in it, as if conspiring. The one lone traffic light at the end of Plumas Street had ceased to go from green to red to green and was blinking a repetitive yellow.

Dawn was a few hours away when I cut the headlights, turned off the engine, and rolled the car to a perpendicular stop across the driveway. We sat for a minute listening to the silence punctuated by the ticking of the warm engine. I'd been to the Van Horn's house often. They lived right around the corner from me. Ken and I were friends who shared a mutual passion for films and music—a lot of Broadway shows with the original casts, Tchaikovsky, Rachmaninoff, sultry Julie London, froggy Lotte Lenya. But I had never been there at that hour of the night. Never at the three a.m. of my soul.

Bridge Street was empty in both directions. The evenly spaced streetlights cast hazy laminations over the pavement in helpless circles beneath the black poles. The camphor trees that lined the street stirred in a breeze with cautionary restlessness, like someone trying to sleep. Black windows stared at us from the house, filled with accusation, as if questioning our arrival and wondering what we were doing there at this hour.

We sat uneasily, as if what we were about to do was a mistake that we'd later regret. To his chagrin, Ken had lost the draw. Pulled the short straw. That was the deal—short straw, your house. Better his than mine and better his than Jack's. It seemed like neutral territory for the next scenario, whatever it was and however it was to be played.

"Okay," Ken had said when he got the short straw, "but George was already half swacked when I left. If we wake him up, he'll be on a rampage." He always called his father by his first name, and his mother too—Evelyn.

We got out of the car. In the cold air, a shiver ran through me. My teeth clattered like castanets and then stopped. I remembered the old wives' tale about when your teeth did that: someone has just walked over your grave. An omen of some kind?

I pictured Ken's room with us in it and the one double bed. The question was, would we be using it? If so, how? What about the back-seat kerfuffle? My boner? His arm? The look on his face? And mine? Questions collided with each other. Plus, it was April, the beginning of spring. Expectations are raised. Everything stirs. Buds swell.

The car doors closed with dull clicks as we leaned into them, as bodies do to muffle the sound, and we walked in single file up the driveway—Ken, then me, then Jack. We entered the house through the back door, tiptoed in the dark through the small laundry room, and made a quick right into the bedroom. George's snoring rattled down the hall from the bedroom at the other end.

We shuffled in the dark as you do when walking blind. Jack stumbled over his own feet and lurched into me and, to catch his balance, grabbed my waist. He pulled me close, then closer. "Oops," he whispered, his warm breath like a reassurance on the back of my neck. What happened next was more complex than anything I'd experienced.

The vacuum caused by the door closing behind us stirred the curtain panels, lifting them from the walls like startled ladies caught sharing naughty secrets. They fluttered among themselves and settled back, demure as proper ladies would be. The ceiling light, bright and alarming, exposed the awkward postures we had assumed in a space that was small and tight, the glare disorienting and feeling like a police lineup until our eyes adjusted. Jack's gaze caught mine. I noticed a look on his face I'd seen earlier, but there was something else, like the insinuation of a conspiracy, one that excluded Ken, who was as close to him as I was, but somehow registering as part of the background, like a figure in the back row of the theater. Jack scanned the room, paused briefly on the bed, grinned. The air sparked; static electricity was palpable and had followed us from the back seat into the room like a fourth party. I knew it. Jack knew it. And Ken knew it. He also knew he was not a part of it.

Time stalled as it had that first day I had stepped into Bobby's house and saw him naked. We were all appraising, processing, deciding.

What do we do now? My dick stirred and twisted in my underwear, pushing against my jeans, restless, needy. Part of me wanted Jack to notice. Another part was terrified he might.

Ken turned on the small bedside table lamp and switched off the ceiling light. A veil was drawn across the room, leaving nuanced shadows that blurred outlines, easing tension while giving gravity to objects they fell from, creating that liminal zone of possibility where one thing becomes another. All the easier to feel the sexual energy and Jack's intention emanating in the semi-dark reaching for me. I imagined what his penis would look like stirring in silk underwear.

<hr>

The furniture in the house was old but not old enough to be antique. Depression-era stuff. Dead people's things. A photo of Karl, Ken's older brother, himself dead two years, was on the dresser watching us, skeptical in his smile, as if he had survived the fatal forklift accident that had killed him a few summers ago when he worked at the Del Monte peach canning factory. Now he was a passive onlooker from the confines of an eight-by-ten frame.

The wall of the neighboring house, owned by Herb Brown, who owned and operated Herb's Standard Station on Plumas Street, and his wife, Thelma, was just outside the bedroom window only about ten feet away beyond a white picket fence trellised with night-blooming jasmine. (Their house was directly in back of ours. Thelma and my mother would visit over the picket fence when they hung out their wash.) The wall was heavy with blossoms, weighing down the trellis it clung to, the syrupy scent invading with a heady aroma, dizzying and seductive. A night bird tested our audience with a handful of repeated notes, like the trill of a flute, alarmed as if calling to a lost mate. Through the folds of the reticulated curtains, spring clouds scudded across the moon, hinting at possible showers and extended thin fingers of useless light through the pattern, nervous and sporadic, giving the landscape of the room the mystery of a brooding watercolor or a dimly lit Caravaggio. Outside in the damp grass, the chirr of crickets rubbing their wings together in hit-and-miss cacophony. The keening of a garden frog stopped to listen and appraise.

Dawn was not far away. Before long, darkness would melt into Creamsicle-colored light, leaving little time to make good the promise of *Later*, if it were going to happen. Everything Jack had done up to then might have simply been a tease. I wouldn't have put it past him.

The room was not prepared. There was nothing to sit on—not a chair or a stool. Being teenagers, at that point we might have done a number of things: two of us lying on the bed and one sitting on the floor, maybe cross-legged; or one on the bed, two on the floor; or even three on the bed. With our clothes on. This is not what happened. It was not clear to me then, and not entirely clear to me now, but an assumption seemed to hang in the air: we'd undress and get in bed. Which is what we did. And as we undressed, we came face to face with our individual and very different hang-ups.

Ken was a fat kid—morbidly obese in today's words, a description you didn't hear in the 1950s. Everyone knew him and liked him, and he was just "chubby." During our friendship, one that lasted decades, I came to understand his complexes, if it's possible to understand someone else's pathology. His was textbook emotional baggage: a middle child emotionally sandwiched between his older brother, Karl, and his younger sister, Patricia. His brother's death had traumatized him far beyond the loss itself. As it happened, he had overheard his mother's hysteria when she was given the news that Karl had been killed. She shrieked, fell to the floor on her knees, her face in an unrecognizable contortion, turned upward in an anguished cry as she wailed, "Why couldn't it have been one of the others?" The Del Monte representatives, two men who had arrived at the front door in somber suits to deliver the news, stood with hats in hand staring at the floor.

In the shock of that moment, Ken thought "one of the others" meant either him or Pat, though it meant one of the other workers at the cannery, a distinction that was never clarified or referred to again. The silences that engulfed him and his Southern Baptist family extinguished any further discussion. Suffering was private. Grief was isolating. I understood. When Ken and I were in our forties, we completed Werner Erhard's Est training together. It was then that he finally shared this part of his family history with me. (Est training was a self-awareness, psycho-babble fad that swept the country at that time.

Ken's misinterpretation shattered his already fragile middle-child sense of self-worth, and he became one of the many who are unable to heal the emotional damage they've suffered. And so, he ate. And later, as he got older, he drank. The addiction to food segued into an addiction to alcohol, the two vacillating back and forth for as long as I knew him. His battle with them was successful for a time and for a time not, for the rest of his life. He was programmed to fail. And he did.

Caption: Ken Van Horn, Carol Petterle, Laurie Michaels, and me at
Top of the Mark, Mark Hopkins Hotel, San Francisco, circa 1962.

My hang-up had a different contortion. Family culture and, to a greater extent, Nazarene Christianity had carved convolutions in my head. My family lived in silences similar to the Van Horns. Our roots were fundamentalist and, to a lesser extent, Catholic— New World hypocrisy and old-world dogma where everyone was handed braces for their brain. Emotions were unshared, stifled, natural urges demonized. Southern Baptist, Nazarene, Catholic, Methodist—all the same. Platitudes and more platitudes. Mumbo jumbo. And guilt. Lots of guilt. The bedrock of Western religion. Our booby prizes.

I learned modesty toward the body—mine and everybody else's—a mantra. So preached the church in word and deed. Nakedness fostered sin and in any form was *verboten*. I also languished with the image of Bobby planted firmly in my head. My scrawny five-year-old physique next to Bobby's washboard belly, cantaloupe ass, and what I saw at the time as a hundred-pound peter. I drew comparison from this for many years as a source of self-perpetuating insecurity. It clung to my brain like a needy child.

Jack's pathology was different still. His birthmark, uncommonly large, took on a psychological dimension that dwarfed its physical size, the dark reddish-purple mass covering an area from just below his waist near the hip bone, curving up across part of his stomach, stopping just under the armpit. Even on the hottest, sweatiest 110-degree days when everybody—fat kids, Ken included—stripped to the waist, Jack never took off his shirt.

In Ken's small room, these issues screamed at us, each within our own heads, while we waited to see who would make the first move—and what that move would be.

"Shouldn't we try to get a little shut-eye?" Ken asked.

Jack and I looked at each other. "I, uh, guess," I stammered.

"Sure. Why not?" Jack added.

Ken pulled two pairs of pajamas from the dresser drawer, holding one pair toward us. "These were Karl's. Share them, if you want. Or not," he said.

I was immediately struck by the fabric—a Western design—and had a lapse into temporary fadeout. *The desert, the cowboys, the horse heads and bucking broncos. The summer, the heat, the sex, so easy and so often.*

It was no surprise that Jack took the top. Snatched it out of Ken's hands. I took the bottom. The three of us turned in opposite directions to undress. As I unbuttoned my shirt, I visualized Jack unbuttoning his, one button at a time, parting in a V, slowly revealing the flesh of his chest. My imagination continued down to his crotch. If either one commented on my semi-erection when we turned around, I'd deal with it then. However, when we did, the sight in front of Ken and me stopped us flat.

The pajama top was too small. The sleeves hit inches above the wrist; the length covered his birthmark but exposed three-quarters of his jockey shorts where a bulge was revealed, leaving little room for imagination. The outline of his sex was clear—a veiny member that pushed insistently against the cloth. I couldn't *not* stare, and my thoughts went back to Bobby naked. His cock had looked as insistent as this one when I followed him into the desert.

With his birthmark covered, Jack relaxed, amused that he had orchestrated such discomfort in Ken and me. How we squirmed at his provocative presentation. Our eyes met, Jack's and mine, and he let his hand slide into his underpants and scratch the thatch of pubic hair. I could almost hear his nails rasp through the wiry thicket. Remembering Bobby's body language that day, this, although different from Bobby, seemed to be a clear invitation. Jack's hand in his underwear and his eyes locked on mine were transmitting what he was thinking—*planning?* And an acknowledgment passed between us—I could feel it, almost touch it. As from one adulterer to another when in mixed company, their tumescence hangs in the air and a covert invitation has been extended. It was also like an unexpected discovery, private and fresh, and in some way acknowledging the aura of sex permeating the room like a dense, rich, and explosive secret.

"I don't know about you two, but I've got to get some sleep," Ken said and turned back the covers as if holding a car door and asking us to get in.

"Oh-kay," Jack said and climbed to the far side. I followed. Then Ken. As the word suggests, a double bed is designed for two, not three, and especially if a third is the fat kid. So, there we were, like pickles in a jar, our complexes, intentions, and expectations under the covers.

Ken smelled of Pall Mall cigarettes; despite usual dishevelment, Jack smelled as if he'd just stepped out of the shower. I didn't smell so fresh—the sweating thing. Despite my lustful thoughts and semi-arousal, and the fact that I was where I'd always wanted to be, I wished I was home in my own double bed.

Ken turned on his side and in a number of deep breaths started to snore, quietly at first, then louder. Sleep had always been quick and profound for him, so unlike me. Jack, also with his back to me, lay with the subtle stillness of the watchfully awake. He was statically aware.

As a blind person will tell you, sounds and smells grow acute in the dark. The closeness of our bodies, the claustrophobic nature of it, heightened my senses to a disproportionate, nearly unnatural degree. I heard the curtains billow in and out, sighing to themselves, lifting away from the walls in gossamer folds of quiet approval. Rain clouds that had teased the sky with a possible spring shower deferred to a starrier sky while other clouds shifted across the moon as if they were changing their minds. Blue-white moonlight threw uneven shadows across the lumpy landscape we created.

Sleep was not in the cards for me. I knew that. With only inches separating us, I felt like Godot's Estragon sandwiched in an awkward place, nowhere to go, waiting, waiting, waiting. Nothing to be done. Wondering, *Is he awake?*

The next segment dragged on in what seemed like hours, probably ten minutes or so by the clock. Then Jack's leg slid slowly across the small distance of sheet and touched mine, or almost did, barely enough to spread the coarse dark hair on my calf with the soft blonde hair of his. From this moment forward, time was filled with potential. At first, I was paralyzed, dry mouthed, my heart pumping against my ribcage. *Was he just changing positions? Or was it intentional? Premeditated? Or involuntary, as in a dream?* No. He wasn't asleep. I could feel it. The question was: *What do I do now? Reciprocate?* Pivotal, this moment was. An impulse could cost—what?—everything, like the Rad Dwyer affair. I was where I'd wanted, but . . . *Now, what the fuck do I do?*

"DO SOMETHING! EVEN IF IT'S WRONG!" A plea from a desperate voice. Desire versus everything else.

"DON'T MOVE!"

"ISN'T THIS WHAT YOU'VE BEEN WAITING FOR? YOU'RE HARD AS A ROCK! YOU KNOW HE IS TOO!"

"WHAT IF I'M WRONG?"

"YOUR WORD AGAINST HIS!"

"I'D NEVER BE ABLE TO EXPLAIN IT! REMEMBER RAD DWYER? HOW PEOPLE LOOKED AT HIM AFTER THAT?"

"THIS IS YOUR CHANCE. MAYBE YOUR LAST!"

It was a chance I had to take. I slid my calf against his, with added pressure, but only slightly. And waited, breathing in rapid, shallow spurts. Air was sucked out of the room and we lay in a giant vacuum. There was no response. Until . . .

His leg moved against mine gently—an affirmation and a questioning caress. Then, with skin on skin, questions held their own answers
and, as if by something transcendental, a vernacular of breath and
silence and touch emerged and became a language where emotions
passed back and forth with a genderless fluidity absent of carnality.
We were not two boys, two males, just two beings in a place there'd
be no coming back from. We'd begun a bewildering slow dance, a
pavane of repression and desire, repeated and repeated, the innocence of which would haunt me through my twenties, my thirties,
my forties, and beyond.

I turned onto my side, lying along the length of his body, coupling
with him as a curvilinear spoon, our legs slightly bent, not completely
together, but barely apart, like quivering birds with strange wings,
trembling and motionless, poised airborne for flight too precarious
to imagine. Blood burned around my heart and desire shimmered,
bending and changing from one incandescent color to another, like
light streaming through a crystal prism, feint and hesitation taking
on the insinuation of a primal mating ritual.

The breeze from the window filled the room with jasmine and
carried the sound of the crickets and the sorrowful notes of that
same bird. The music of the outside world was becoming alerted to
a noiseless dawn not far away. The sound shifted, quieted, retreated.
The air lost signs of movement, became still, contemplating the conse-
quences of daylight.

I have no idea of how much time had passed. Our bodies had gone
beyond the confines of the clock. The moon was dropping from the
sky, paling the stars as the first signs of morning arrived in the colors
that slowly bled one into the other. The day was crawling toward

us, making its way over the sill and into the room. Ken snorted and stirred. From the dresser, Karl's eyes, unable to see us in the dark, watched in the emerging light, regarding us through sepia colors. The moon, cruelly serene, was ready to take its leave. Time, mutable as always, killer of mood and fantasy, had moved forward and had run out. The imminence of daylight twisted the panic in my stomach first into fluttering wings and then into a knot.

"Not yet," I pleaded to no one, to God. Neither fear nor desire had finished with me. Pleasure was still in the luxury of delay. I needed confirmation. Of what? Fear swelled into a living organism, slippery and deaf to reason and left me teetering on the ledge of recklessness, not able to talk myself down.

I pressed the full length of my body into Jack's curved backside, the tip of my cock straining above the waistband of my underwear. A warm emission in even spurts oozed out and spread, wetting the curve of his lower back. He made a sound, almost too quiet to hear. As he did, his head turned sideways, as if grasping for my face. In the fixed, hollow, opened mouth, his thoughts were cast. Regret? Repulsion? Ecstasy? It was impossible to tell. Whatever it was, it wasn't good. I knew that.

Like a flash of lightening on a black ocean, I knew I'd made a mistake. Had misread, misjudged. As Jack turned his head away from me, my only feeling was remorse—deep, dark, ugly, and irretrievable. And the fucking voices. *We told you.*

Jack showed signs of waking with an exaggeration of yawning and stretching that would convince no one. Certainly not me. Ken twitched, coughed, stumbled out of bed clearly having come from a deep sleep. I rolled onto my back with shame weighing so heavily on my innards I felt I couldn't get up. *What the fuck have I done?* There was no going back and no way out.

We dressed as we had undressed, the silence filling the spaces, different than it had been, reverberating loud now, ringing, peeling remorse, embarrassment, confusion. *What do I do now?*

Outside, light gray would turn pink, then red, orange, and finally in the bright yellow of the day, blue would cap the clear spring sky and the day would fill with its own pleasures but now more like a fading light than the break of dawn—an ending rather than a beginning. Irrevocable. The bird was gone, the cricket sounding more like a rusty hinge than a musical accompaniment. Walking to the car, the air was misty, as if it had just stopped crying. Dawn stepped aside for daylight. We climbed into the car. Jack's face was as grim as I had ever seen it, but more so—blank, unresponsive, and unreadable.

The cum had seeped into my underwear and been absorbed, cold and wet and sticking to the skin through my pubic hair, an acrid reminder as we drove to the Buttes, its smell intermingled with my remorse.

We drove to Sunrise Service as if it were a duty no one wanted to honor, nothing more than an exercise in futility. Ken sat next to me in front; Jack was in the back. A light mist, only a pitiful drizzle, sheeted the windshield as we climbed the winding country road and the tires whirred on the wet pavement. We watched the Easter service from the car in silence for a few minutes with the motor running, the sound of the engine purring under the flap-flap of the windshield wipers. I put the car in reverse quietly and gently, as if we were leaving a memorial service, turned it around, and headed back to town on the narrow, two-lane country road, trying to keep my mind on anything other than what it kept going back to. But the enigmatic look on his face when he turned his head toward me in the half darkness, the open mouth, the wild, questioning eyes, flashed like an angry intrusion and continued to derail any darting thoughts I tried to distract myself with.

The farmland that stretched before us was devoid of life or line or movement and looked as if it had been painted on a canvas, not really real. It lay, wet and dark, as if nighttime were spread out in a horizontal plane. My eyes, troubled and brooding, having no other eyes to connect with, looked straight ahead past the black fields and into the blinding rays of the rising sun as it inched up from the skyline intruding on the new day. The half-arc of a rainbow cut through the sky, failing to find earth.

Ken tried to lift the dark mood, a fourth passenger in the car, with the signature humor that usually worked so well for him, each attempt falling flatter than the one before, finally giving up beating that distinctly dead horse. I kept my thoughts to myself (there was nowhere else to put them) while Jack stared out the window with his chin weighing heavily on his fist. *What was he thinking? Had he discovered feelings he had to deny? Or regret? Or be terrified of?* Distraught questions assaulted me during the long stretch of wet country road whirring under the tires.

I dropped Ken off at his house and drove Jack to his. The silence gained weight with each street, each block, each intersection, the distance between us accumulating, the tension mounting. He stepped out of the car into a shallow puddle of water, disrupting a patch of sky reflected there. Over his shoulder he said, walking away, "Sometimes you just have to hold back." I have never been able to forget this. Nor decode the exact meaning.

An apology? A confession? A criticism? A warning? I watched him disappear around the backside of the house and listened to a siren wail, diminishing in the distance. The drizzle was gone and the sky by then had become unbearably blue and brilliant.

As the years have passed, I have tried to put the experience into words but found all lacking. Even now, words feel inadequate. How do you describe that second when the physical and the spiritual fuse? When two bodies emerge as if from one chrysalis? When two souls feel as one? And then, as surely as it came, disappear in seconds?

—————

Jack and I drifted apart at school; the connection we'd had became a wedge. Never could he look me in the face if we happened to cross paths. A new kind of silence sharpened between us, one laced with thoughts and feelings that could never be articulated. The closeness I felt—thought—we had disappeared, as if it had just been a figment of my imagination. A fabrication I had fashioned. Something out of nothing. The feelings I had held precious were gone. We left high school after graduation and lived lives as different as we ourselves were and were to become.

There was, of course, no claim I could lay on him, just as the present has no claim on the future—only the assurance that it will in time be the past. Still, as claimless as our relationship was, rage and rejection and grief were not. Those were mine and were deeply staked into my heart. Sadness, compromised and censored for want of sharing it with someone, weighed down on my shoulders. Then came numbness, like the kind that comes from an injury, before pain starts to make its way through. Resentment festered beneath the pride under which I concealed it. I couldn't fathom feeling any other way. Still, *if only I'd . . .*

Jack started dating a perky cheerleader with a gold cap on her front tooth, as proud to show it off as he was paranoid about hiding his birthmark, an irony not lost on me. In a few weeks, his class ring hung around her neck. *Going steady* was only a short step away from an engagement ring. This was the rumor. They clung together arm in arm, whispering in quiet exchanges, clearly besotted with the paralysis of young love, still in those blissful hours before you truly know one another. It all seemed to come so easily to him and perfectly naturally (all the more galling). Their behavior had the short fuse of carnal dynamite. I imagined they were fucking a lot. I cursed myself. *How could I have been such a fool?* I had lost myself in him, as I had with Bobby. I wanted his life ruined, soiled, damaged, and dismembered as his rejection had ruined, soiled, and damaged me.

Distress leveled out, as it does in time. And revenge, if that's what it was, came ten or twelve years later. I mailed him a book I had read in senior English class—*Raintree County*, an allegory about an illusory end to a fraught emotional journey. A beautiful girl goes mad and dies at the loss of an unrequited love. At the end, she's found under the broad branches of the raintree, having wandered through the woods lost and deranged. The raintree had leaves of gold—an allusion to an illusion.

On the inside cover, I inscribed, "for you in silence, from somewhere in the fifties," and left it unsigned. Would he puzzle over it, the meaning and the source? Would his wife thumb through the book, see the inscription, and ask, "Who was 'in silence from the fifties'?" Would that question ignite a flicker of recognition? Or later, laying sleepless, would he continue to wonder? Ask himself questions? Maybe realize it had come from me?

From time to time, I have entertained a fantasy where Jack has somehow followed my life and career from afar, using me as a benchmark to measure his own life—what he'd done and hadn't done, what he'd accomplished, and what he'd been unable to acknowledge. Then I regretted sending the book at all. But aren't we, in part, made of things we regret? *What a fool,* I thought. In some ways, I'm still the same fool. Still, even as I write this, I can feel his breath on the back of my neck. *If only I'd . . .*

Thoughts of him return, uninvited, as they do with Bobby. Fragments attended by fits of sadness, rage, or exhilaration, as if it all happened yesterday but striking today like a bolt of lightning. And then gone. None fitting neatly into any one place. Writing about it makes the experience feel more concrete only in the delusional way taking pen to paper offers the assumption of permanence.

Most of this has faded now, has become sepia-colored like Karl's old photograph. I've had to make room for other disappointments, other feelings. Still, I can't help but wonder if all that happened in high school was just that—what happened in high school. Was the idea that it was something more nothing but a product of a presumptive imagination? An exaggerated poetic conceit? My sense of entitlement? It was, to be sure, a time when I wanted too much of everything. (But don't I always? Still?) Or could it really have been what it felt like at the time—love on the highest level? Even in the uncertainty, I do like to revisit the moonlight, the lace curtains, the anticipation, the tension, the release, even the regret. I see it from far away, as if it had been someone else's experience or had been felt in a dream. I knew I would write about it someday with, perhaps, a fitting epigraph from Henry James. "We love as we must, not as we should." Melodramatic and overwrought? Yes, I'm still that too.

I have to laugh at one silly thing I said to myself as he walked to his back door: "I want to die." But people only die of love in the movies. Harsh feelings dissipate. They stop being the only things you feel. They fade. Make room for other things. You survive, but not exactly. And then, as Proust said, so it happens that the memory of things "comes often, but for shorter intervals of time, like an addict being withdrawn slowly from a drug." I've come to learn that some delusions are necessary for love. How many is impossible to say, for, after all, the heart has more chambers than we can see, pumping where emotion replaces blood, hidden and mysterious and, as Ezra Pound says, "There is no end of things in the heart."

And you can never duplicate the first time. There is ever only one, forever overshadowed by what Edmund White calls "the exquisite melancholy of parting." But my *saudade,* the genetic makeup of the inescapable, dictated that I search for those same feelings in other times and other places, a search that ends like a concert in the park, dying when the music stops, Mozart disappearing in thin air.

CHAPTER 7

THE KEY

S ECRETS IN HIGH SCHOOL were rarely secrets long. The fact that I had the key to the house of Mr. Roy, the school's Spanish teacher, in the pocket of my Levi's was no exception. Word of it traveled, like all rumors did, as I have said before, at a speed second only to the speed of light. The small brass object, so ordinary when taken at face value, not only opened the door to Mr. Roy's house but also closed the door on a fact of my life more significant than what such a small object should have the power to.

It took on a disproportionate notoriety by virtue of the person to whom it belonged and the person to whom it had been given. The news that I had it spread like wildfire, fanned by gossiping girls (and boys) in Mr. Roy's classroom and soon on to more far-flung ears. Overnight, I became the subject of ribbing and had to stammer through sweaty palms and multiple denials. "You're *so* magnanimous," my friends teased. Magnanimous was Mr. Roy's word for me. He used similar adjectives on a few others.

"Okay, so I'm magnanimous. So what? I don't even know what that word means! And anyway, Trent's a "prince"!

That didn't stop the teasing. "So, you and fruity Andre, huh?"

"What the fuck's that supposed to mean?" I snapped, a guilty response where there was, in fact, no guilt. What was I supposed to say?

Mr. Roy had allowed me the use of the small, one-bedroom bungalow he rented on Palm Street, just blocks from school. I had his permission (and a kind of blessing but with a caveat) to use it at my discretion during Christmas vacation while he was in San Francisco on a different kind of holiday—the kind of Bay Area disappearing act I learned about several years after high school when I accidentally ran into a former student of his, one of those awkward moments where you turn a corner and run into someone you'd rather not have. I'll call this person *Bill*, since I couldn't remember his name when we met and still can't. What I do remember is that Bill had a very sibilant voice and walked a fine line of flamboyancy that was right on the cusp of being unacceptable behavior in Yuba City, particularly if he were sss-sibiling near the town toughs. The information he had offered in an effusive, colorful, dramatic, certainly fey way suggested they'd once had a close, maybe very close, relationship. How close was more information than I wanted or needed to hear and more than Bill offered? I just assumed that he assumed that I would assume what I would.

He blathered on, jumping from one subject to another, his limp wrists loosely connecting his trains of thought. Through his performance (and it was indeed a performance), I was able to glean the meat of Mr. Roy's San Francisco weekends. He spent a lot of time in a well-known gay bar, the Black Cat, a fully packed, smoke-filled dive in the financial district where a petite Mexican queen whose name was Jose—but everyone called "Josie"—in tight black pants and a long braid down his back would stand on the top of the bar and sing arias from *Carmen* in a voice too high to be masculine, too low to be feminine, to an audience of drinking, smoking, cruising men.

At the time that I heard the story from Bill, I had left UC campus at Berkeley and was living in San Francisco, struggling with an intense, if short-lived, dance career, my *brisé volé* in the Bluebird solo from the Sleeping Beauty never close to par. This was at a time when every aspiring male dancer held Rudolph Nureyev, who had recently defected from the Russian Bolshoi to England's Royal Ballet, as the ultimate male ballet dancer.

I'd been to the Black Cat a couple of times myself and found it hard to imagine Mr. Roy there. I couldn't picture him as Black Cat material.

What Mr. Roy did in and out of town had always been a subject for speculation, but no one ever knew for sure what he did or didn't do. Bill had filled in a lot of the holes. He and Mr. Roy went to gay bars. But in high school, "Gay bar? What's a gay bar?" Fairy. Queer. Yes. Gay. No. I can't remember exactly when the word became part of my vocabulary.

Humpty-Dumpty shaped Mr. Roy. Mr. E. Andre Roy. (What the *E* stood for we never knew. It could have been Ed. Or Earl. "Or Edna," we joked.) He flounced into his Spanish classes overdosed in heavy, ruttish cologne. An older, unshaven, pear-shaped figure in clingy Hawaiian shirts, like nylon slips, untucked, out from which his stomach urged and wearing the same trousers day after day that were wrinkled like a big stack of smiles. He wore bolo ties and half-glasses that hung like a lorgnette on a chain around his neck or perched on the end of his nose as he peered over them while conjugating verbs in Spanish I, II, and III classes. He was enormously popular with the students, and in his introductory speech the first day he declared that he would henceforth be "holding court" (translation: teaching) in Castilian Spanish which he pronounced "Cath-sthillian." "Prepare yourselves, because I'll be speaking Spanish a lot in here. You'll have to haul ass to keep up," another pronouncement he made at the same time. It wasn't true. Nobody worked hard in Spanish. It was an easy language with an even easier teacher.

Me and Mimi Janislowski in Coppélia, *1964.*

San Francisco, circa 1964.

He thrived on double entendres and found a way of injecting them into the lesson one way or another, like conjugating a verb so as to make it sound nearly prurient: "*Yo excito, tú excitas, nosotros excitamos,*" he'd say with pouty lips, a lifted chin, and one raised eyebrow, finger-ing the glasses around his neck as if they were a body part. As you might expect, this created chaos, particularly if a class jock picked up the ball, grabbed his crotch, and repeated, "Yo excito, yo excito," prompting the rest of the class to chant in unison, "Yo excito, yo excito" and kept it up until Mr. Roy stepped in, laughing, holding both hands up at forty-five degrees and patting the air. "Okay, okay. That's enough, you folks. That's enough. Settle down. Let me finish." He enjoyed the deviation as much as the students, particularly the grabbing of the crotch part. Probably more so.

He spoke Spanish off and on to the class, as promised, rolling his Rs and his eyes, pronouncing "s" as "th," and then had the class repeat, or try to repeat, what he'd said. Then he would translate. In hindsight, the technique wasn't such a bad one. Being spoken to in the language day to day and then saying the words out loud—a lot was absorbed by rudimentary osmosis.

Mixed in with *adjectivos, adverbios,* and *preposiciones,* class lectures were chock-full of barbs and sarcasms aimed mostly at the rural valley town we lived in, which, according to Mr. Roy, was a cultural waste-land inhabited by "peach pickers" and "bean eaters," sarcasms that settled into lines on his face. Excluded from these barbs were his pets, his favorite students, mostly male and by all accounts good-looking, for whom adjectives took a loftier turn. I was "magnanimous." Trent Thompson was "a prince." And so forth. The fact that he cut lots of slack over late assignments and handed out A grades with abandon made his class very popular. Holding court with outrageous comments and semi-salacious stories came first for him. Imparting the particu-lars of the Spanish language, second.

The classroom was a rickety Quonset hut with creaky floors. It was hard to heat and located at the far edge of the campus, which I thought of as a comment on what the school administration thought of him. Or chose not to. Fortunately, he had tenure.

My later contacts with other men of his type and temperament found that he had not been so very different from many old fairies of exaggerated sighs and over-splashed colognes I came to know, personalities that were moderately entertaining at first and then became *de trop* and tiresome.

———

"Don't do anything I wouldn't do," Mr. Roy chortled that last Friday after class, a perverse grin spreading over his five o'clock shadow. As he handed me the key, he glanced left, right, then left again, as if someone seeing our "deal" would assume something untoward between us was going on, a caution I thought extreme since we were the only two left in the room.

The handshake that had sealed the deal was creepy and almost suggestive of an embrace or a caress, his soft, limp fingers lightly wrapped around mine with a grip that was as soft and creepy as Mr. Reeves's had been tight and greasy. An arched eyebrow notarized the transaction, and, as he stared me in the face and nodded up and down, I knew he expected a full report after the fact. The cost of doing business. He loved gossip as much as any schoolgirl.

The tiny house was on a narrow street that was more like an alley. The neighbors were primarily elderly couples who went to bed early and could only crane their necks and speculate what was going on with that unmarried high school teacher who took out the trash once a week and left town on the Greyhound bus most weekends. It was a dark and quiet location.

Mr. Roy's house was going to be our pit stop to sober up in before going home. There would be five of us: Craig Osborne, Trent Thompson, Jerry Newberg, and me, and a wild card named Mari (pronounced "Ma-REE," with a heavy emphasis on the "Ree," like the character Cherie, pronounced "Che-REE" (same emphasis on the last syllable) in *Bus Stop*. Mari thought this affectation gave her a touch of class. It didn't.

Mari Montrose was her full name. ("We're French.") She was the only girl coming with us. This alone was a red flag. I missed it. Mari was never included in any socializing we did either in or out of school and, of all the girls we knew, she should have been the very last to have been invited. Plus, beer busts were traditionally guys only. That, too, should have told me something.

At an Amazonian six-foot-one, Mari cut a wide swath, as wide as her hips, with her own brand of virtue and vice and behavior as intimidating as it was vulgar, like the habit she had of spitting through the wide space between her two front teeth. Angry and out of a bottle, her electric blonde hair curled in a "Don't fuck with me" way, underscoring her "Don't fuck with me" attitude.

Flip-flops, which she wore no matter the occasion, slapped annoyingly against the bottoms of her feet, inconsistent with the fifty-cent pearls she wore every day. Discounting the unfortunate way she dressed, it was pretty clear she had the kind of body that would never wear clothes well under any circumstance. Even so, I had to admit a certain admiration for Mari. Her white trash style and unfettered behavior lacked moral baggage, which gave her the touch of class she believed came solely from the way she pronounced her name. She rarely judged anyone unkindly but could embarrass the shit out of them at the same time, never passing up the chance to mock or deride. At the same time, a streak of kindness and generosity ran through her—not untypical, as I've observed, in those from the wrong side of the tracks, and like those with the least to always give the most.

Mari lived at the intersection of hot and crazy with, as that ad says, just the right amount of wrong, and was proud of the reputation she had as a real ballbuster. However, I'd have to say she was *halfway decent*, a phrase I picked up from my father. I have no idea exactly what "halfway decent" meant in his terms. I just knew deep down she wasn't a bad sort.

"If Mari had as many dicks sticking out of her as in, she'd look like a fucking porcupine," an observation she herself laughed at. But there was no hard evidence to support this, unless she was fucking the off-duty Beale Air Force Base soldiers who hung out at the bar in the Olympic Hotel, a broken-down dive in Marysville. That was a possibility.

"Still jerkin' off in the john, Willy?" she cracked to Willy Williamson, a nerdy guy and an easy butt of jokes. He wore his pants hiked up three inches above his waist, the same way he wore his gym shorts, and was often seen talking to himself because nobody else would. Guys from the boys' john reported that they heard the sound of skin slapping skin from behind the locked door of his stall. He was sitting in there longer than any reasonable dump would take—a dead giveaway.

Mari's remark turned him scarlet, as she knew it would, and left him mumbling to himself as he slinked away. Her talent for finding everyone's weak spot was unrivaled. If you were easily embarrassed, you steered clear.

"I can just watch him walk down the hall and cream my jeans," she said in a voice that could be heard within a fifty-foot radius. The *him* was me. She had major hots for me, another not-so-secret secret.

Several days before the party, a trail of clues had been dropped like breadcrumbs in the forest. There were also plenty of innuendos that a joke was going to be played—on me. With the credence I gave to subtle remarks, especially when it might involve me or my feelings, I should have picked up on them, but didn't. How I missed it, I'll never know. I should have seen what was coming.

I assumed Mari had been invited for entertainment value. She was a terrific whipping post, giving back as good as she got—better, in fact, volleying wisecracks back like an ace ping-pong player. Being the only girl in a group of good-looking, popular guys, especially if it included the guy she could cream her jeans over, would be an opportunity she wouldn't miss, given the chance.

Maybe Craig, Trent, and Jerry assumed I had figured it out. I was going to be the fall guy and was going to play along, good sport that I was. On the other hand, they also should have known that I was never a good sport when it was at my own expense. Whatever the truth was, the party went ahead as planned.

The end of the year meant the beginning of that dead part of winter, the bleak stretch of corrosive weather between January and March—ghostly, dormant months when fog rolls in and old people lose the will to live. Even in the icy and unforgiving air, there was something beautiful about that particular time of year, if only in a bleak, heart-broken kind of way.

I looked forward to Christmas. Dreaded it, too, for its unyielding, unending good cheer with decorations strung in every store window in Marysville and Yuba City, garish and redundant, making the holiday itself garish and redundant. The closer Christmas got, the more saturated with Christmas music the radio waves became. The ornaments, the tinsel, the holly, the many mangers, the many babes in swaddling clothes and variations of Santa Claus—all of it so tinseled and festooned that the spirit of Christmas was tarnished with the weight of its own decoration.

But even back then, with every version of every carol on every radio station, herald angels harking on every radio station spun me into melancholia, not joy to the world. And the most annoying of all, the Chipmunks singing "Rudolph the Red-Nosed Reindeer," their helium voices grating and painful to the ear. New Year's Eve was always a gigantic relief. I welcomed the stroke of twelve. The next night would finally be silent for real.

The days drew themselves inward in wintertime, bringing the sun low in the fields as the geese flew south, their mournful voices echoing collective goodbyes from the loose V shapes in the gray skies. The trees went bare and the north wind blew with a ferocity that chilled to the bone. Fog, in the slow, nefarious way it moved, seemed to lack conviction in its dank viscosity while still aware of its own power, moving as it did, settling over the valley, camouflaging deadly objects around unexpected curves in the road. Weather advisories said to stay off the roads unless necessary. The dense gray blanket closed the Sacramento airport, and the entire valley lay under the fog like a lonely place of untold secrets.

We were never put off by the weather. A beer party was a beer party no matter what. We drove over the bridge in tandem to Marysville to find Squeaky. He bought beer for teenagers for a small consideration. Three bucks usually. *Squeaky*, short for "Squeaky Clean," was the handle he'd acquired. He was, of course, anything but. What his real name was no one knew or cared to know. He was all about the beer.

We could generally find him in the same back alley in Marysville in the seediest part of old town off 2nd Street right around the corner from the Davis Hotel, a well-known red-light hotel in the town's one-block red-light district. He was always ready to make a buck.

Squeaky was half hobo, half con man, with hair the dull color of a long-circulated nickel. He always needed a bath. By the way he smelled, he hadn't had one in who knew how long. We found him leaning against the wall making conversation with a couple of streetwalkers.

"Hey, Squeaky," I called from the car. "Wanna make a couple bucks?"

He squinted in our direction, recognized us as regular customers, and said, "Yeah, man. Sure. Okay. Wha' chou need?" in a sandpaper voice, followed by a cough of yellow-greenish phlegmy content that he hacked onto the sidewalk with not a shred of compunction. Squeaky was unrefined.

"Some Bud," I said. Beer, not pot. Pot came years later. "Get in."

He leaned in the window to check out the others in the car before climbing into the back seat next to Mari. "How 'bout five bucks and ten minutes with this split tail here?" he said, nodding her way, know-ing the answer before asking the question. He chortled and coughed up the phlegm he had no choice but to swallow.

"In your dreams, asshole," Mari said with a curled but teasing lip.

"How 'bout three and you find your own split tail," I countered, "like one of those fine gals you're talking to?" "Okay." He coughed again, swallowed, chortled, and smiled, a crooked row of brown teeth intruding from behind his thin lips. We drove to Herb Wurtz's Liquor Store, Squeaky smelling up the car so bad we had to roll the windows down in spite of the cold. Herb was standing behind the counter as he always was, tall and thin with hair slicked back over his head, a cigarette hanging out of the corner of his mouth letting the smoke curl up into his nostrils, cadaver-like under the fluorescent light hanging over the counter. I could not for the life of me see what Jetta Flowers, a larger than life "Jamaican" local, found appealing about him even though they had been a reputed item for a long time. Jetta was a local "businesswoman" with no ties to the Better Business Bureau but who was well known in the county welfare department, from whom she received an additional welfare check for each illegitimate child she birthed, several of whom were thought to be Herb's. "When Herb ska' Wurtzs, Jetta flowers." The local joke.

Squeaky made the purchase no questions asked, even though Herb could clearly see us in the car, teenagers but regular customers. Two trips and four six-packs of Budweiser later, Squeaky loaded the beer into the open trunk of the car and climbed back in. Herb gave a half-hearted wave and a knowing nod as we drove off to drop our smelly buyer back in the alley. I handed him three singles over my shoulder, which he counted twice just to make sure. He got out, put a finger to one nostril, and blew a thick clump of snot onto the sidewalk. As we drove away, he had insinuated himself into a trio of skimpily clad ladies talking among themselves with intermittent bronchial coughing who were gathered outside the back entrance to Mama's Place, the popular Chinese restaurant, where skinny alley cats twisted themselves in and out of indigent legs, purring and pleading for a handout.

We headed back over the bridge to the river in the snazzy car I got before my sixteenth birthday. I say *before*. I was only fifteen. Sixteen was the legal age for a driver's license, but back then a teenager of fourteen and a half, if a member of a family farming business, was allowed to drive with only a learner's permit, which I had. The proviso was you had a licensed driver with you, which I never did. (Think back on my father's attitude toward the firstborn son.) A black 1957 Chevrolet convertible with red and silver upholstery cut a very flashy swath around school.

Trent, "the Prince," was in the front seat with me. Craig and Jerry were behind us in another car. We drove back to Yuba City and down Plumas Street, where the spills of light from the top of the poles were muted, bruised emanations, like Baudelaire's Paris. Grayness settled over Yuba City the same way it did in the City of Light. In the moment, the street decorations were eerily festive in the fog.

Once through town, we headed south on the Garden Highway at a speed faster than was safe, ending up on the half-hidden road that led over the levee and down into the river bottoms several miles south of town, the best place for beer parties, well hidden from our nemesis, George Reusser of the Yuba City Police and the people from the ABC (Alcohol Beverage Control). Within the walls of the levee, noise went up, not out. Like the key, the river bottom was a secret everybody knew about. On a night like this, we would probably be the only ones there.

The road up the levee was rutted with remembrance, as was the river bottoms itself. The windshield wipers worked furiously, sluicing the accumulating fog on the glass, flinging it left and right. The car had become stifling with the heater on high and Squeaky's presence. His smell lingered. I cracked my window and breathed in the yellow-brown grasses, wet with dew and smelling of fresh peat.

The two cars crisscrossed the levee and, as we went up and over and down, their beams cut harsh, probing diagonals across the terrain like hunters on a search and rescue. Dead weeds that ran down the middle of the one-lane gravel road scratched the undercarriages like fingers on a blackboard, and bare trees flashed white in the headlights, their limbs, crossed and gnarled, smacking of an underlying conspiracy. I could feel an anxiety building, for two reasons. First, Mari's vibe—"I can just watch him walk down the hall and cream my jeans." And the second, well, there really wasn't a second. Except that something was definitely off.

We had the beer, always a leveler, a smoother of situations. Drink and senses dull. Everything gets fuzzy. Disorientation like that might solve the problem, if it was a problem I was going to have. Still, there was an anticipation sitting high in my chest that was not mollified by the reassuring sound of six-packs rattling and shivering in the trunk. I was afraid that this time beer was not going to be a remedy. Nobody was talking much, not even Mari. That was not a good sign. Trent was grinning. But then, he always grinned too much.

Thickets of trees up and down the riverbank cast no shadow, and the moon hung in place, weak and powerless and half hidden. The darkness was full of noises that told of things happening beyond where they could be seen—secrets but not mysteries. To the east, the lights of Marysville strained through the grisly illumination. The black water was out there not far away, sensed rather than seen, and the riverbed formed a long, narrow bowl that held the gray weather within parallel levees, lucent but opaque.

I had grown tired of my attitude. The suspicions I had were killing whatever good mood I should have been in. It was, after all, supposed to be a party. For the time being, I ignored what my intuition was trying to tell me and said to myself, *This is stupid. It's just a party. Get with the program. Let it go.* That was fully my intention. The night got off to a good start, which made how it ended that much worse.

We pulled into the flats, angling the cars toward each other with the lights on, leaving a campfire of beamed illumination that dissipated onto small, shivering puddles here and there. The radios were turned up and the doors of the cars flung open like seagulls airing their wings so we could listen to Stan's Bandstand, a nine-to-midnight call-in station sponsored by Stan's Drive-In that played requests for three hours with songs dedicated to girlfriend from boyfriend, or boyfriend to girlfriend, confirmations of young love made on KMYC every Saturday night.

"Who's got the church key?" someone asked.

"In the glove compartment. I'll get it," I said.

We pass the opener from person to person, forcing the pointed end into the cans with finesse to avoid a sudden spray of foam spewing. And the party started in the windless, cutting air. We drank and laughed and wobbled on the shifting rocks while the darkness and the fog encircled us. The black of the air waited, marking time, sitting at our periphery. Stark branches of naked bushes here and there jagged through what little light was dismissed from the headlights.

"Next up, Mickey and Silvia with 'Love Is Strange.' Going out to Brad from Lynne, to DeeDee from Tom, to John from Mardelle, and to Bobby from Nancy. Here they are, listeners, Mickey and Silvia and 'Love . . . Is . . . Strange.'" (I remember the words, singing them in my head sometimes, knowing now how much stranger love turned out to be than Mickey and Silvia ever suggested. Sometimes very, very strange.) I listened for "To Jack from Judy" or "To Judy from Jack" but heard neither.

"So, Richie-Boy. What's with you and Edna?" Mari said to me.

"Wadda you mean?" I snarked, knowing exactly what she meant.

"The key thing? You and Andre?" she said, an edge of implication obvious in the way she said it.

"I have no idea what you're talking about," I snarked again, trying to pass it off. I shifted from one foot to the other, feeling suddenly like I was in the sights of a hunter toying with its prey.

"Ah, c'mon. You're *sooo* magnanimous. What's he want, anyway?" she persisted.

"I have no idea what you're talking about," I answered. I did.

"Just sayin'. There's talk." She wasn't going to let it go.

"So?" I said, knowing what she was getting at.

"So, nothin'," she replied. "I just heard—"

"I don't give a shit what you heard. Fuck off, why don't you?" I snorted.

"Okay, okay. Forget it," Mari said apologetically, satisfied that she'd hit a nerve. The others guffawed, too chickenshit to comment. We fell into pregnant pauses where everyone looks around wondering what, if anything, could re-kick-start the mood that had just put a damper on the party. Time for another beer. We had chugged through three of the four cases, drinking too fast for good sense or assimilation, and conversation was made up of what we had said in different ways so many times before, demanding nothing in the way of thought or concentration.

Fuzzy in the head now and knowing that something was up, I still couldn't put my finger on it. I had, however, a strong inkling that it had to do with the blonde giant standing among us. My chest and shoulders tightened the way they can in the cold. Also, in the way they do when you feel wary. Footing was getting worse, words more slurred, jibs more taunting. Lots of "fuck this" and "fuck that" and deflection from what was *sub-rosa*. Camaraderie had turned fickle, more tenuous and less sincere. No one except Mari, as bold as she was, could look me in the eye. She did. With a smirk on her face.

Fuck. Maybe I'm just imagining, I thought. But I could tell we were nearing the tipping point where alcohol can divide friendships. Voids in conversation were deep, too deep to fill, and turned into stale, vacant spaces, and everything comment seemed to border on accusation. Alcohol had spun me to the darker side of my brain where I interpreted everyone and everything as an adversary wielding a confrontation. I disengaged, went to temporary fadeout, and started looking at the five of us as if we were characters in a Beckett play, with connections evaporating. We started talking at, not to, one another, and made stale conversation where there wasn't any.

"Fuckin' freezin' out here," Craig said.

"Pussy," Mari jibed.

"Pussy, my ass," he responded. "I'm still hangin'. But in this kinda weather like a stack of buttons." Everybody laughed but me.

"How 'bout you, Beauty?" Mari directed my way. "You hangin' like that?"

"Fuck you. And the horse you rode in on," I answered, through chattering teeth and slurred words, thinking I was being cool and glib and holding my own. I wasn't. I was literally shaking in my boots.

"Fuck me? Now that's the proposition I was waiting for," she purred.

I had no response for that. But everyone else laughed. I hesitated and then laughed with them, a shiver running down my spine. I stared into the black around me, thinking, *What do I do now?* My mind scuttled around like a rat in a corner.

The air had turned thicker and colder and the tippy rocks more tippy, the unsure footing undercutting conversation. The mood was tentative, as though the tension was in wait—waiting until we were wobbly enough and cold enough to step in and change the souring mood from taut to bad to worse—to that moment where a switch flicks itself on and booze leads to wife-beating or suicide or other bad shit.

Like hot fireflies sparking in non-unison, the cigarettes cast a chiaroscuro glow off and on with each sporadic drag, and a striking match was the only noise for what seemed like minutes. After the last bit of repartee between Craig and Mari and me, each moment became more uncomfortable than the one before it. Mari was as happy as a pig in shit. Trent and Craig and Jerry looked everywhere but at me, refusing to make eye contact—a sure sign of guilt. The more Mari drank, the more provocative her body language became, somehow able to exude hot sexuality on a cold night with a tip of the pelvis, or how she ran her tongue over her lips, or how pulled at panties stuck in the crack of her butt. "Beer makes me so-o-o horny," she purred, as if her sex drive was the totality of who she was.

Words were more than hidden agenda now, and, once again, we are *Waiting for Godot* and I am Estragon, melancholy, bitter, clinging to survival. We were disconnecting, becoming cardboard cutouts. I read hidden meaning into everything and forced myself into that place inside my head, that sanctuary where my voices were free to speak, to judge, to advise. An owl calling clear and questioning from a cottonwood tree asked, "Who? Who?" And then another owl with the same questions, like coded messages. A fox in the distance cried like an abandoned baby.

I flashed to the future, where our lives would be separated for good, erasing this night and all my attendant paranoia. Where would we be? What would we be doing? Our tickets would be punched to different directions, different destinations—college, a job here, if that was where the future was, or directly down the altar into marital oblivion? Craig, Jerry, Trent, and Mari stared off in different directions. What were they thinking? I ached for summer as Elvis's entreaty played on the radio, completely out of touch. *"Love me tender, love me true . . ."*

The cold air constricted my muscles and extended down into my pants pocket where my hand fingered the key. Surely Mari knew about the key—everyone did. Maybe that's why she was getting louder, bolder, ready to bust some balls, crushing beer can after beer can with one hand in a machismo sort of way, as if she wanted to prove she had a bigger pair than the four of us put together. My urge to leave was as strong as the necessity that kept me there. There was no way out. Finally, Craig broke the ice.

"Whadaya say we all have a go attcha, Mari?" he said. With the first card played, I saw where this was going. So did Mari. Her smile said so, as plain as the space between her teeth.

"Good luck gittin' to that party," she laughed, throwing her head back.

"Think you could fuck us all, big girl?" Trent replied.

"Come on, hotshot," she replied, clearly a dare. "Bring it on. I feel like a million, but I'll take your pricks one at a time."

She wasn't Mae West, that's for sure. Not even close. But that's not the point. She had drawn a line in the sand. In the cold, exhaled breath was visible, and I was in a sweat.

Trent's perfectly aligned white teeth, just unwired from three years of metal braces, seemed to glow in the dark when he grinned and said, "You know what they say. Big woman, small hole. Small woman, all hole. You're a pretty big gal, Mari. Is it true? Big girl, small hole?" Trent had that kind of personality. He thought everything he said was clever. He was pretty but not clever. And not even that smart.

"Good luck any of you fillin' my hole, you scrawny little fuckers," she replied, not backing down. "That is if you even know where it is." She cackled. "Except maybe him," tipping her head in my direction. They all grinned.

How dense had I been? The joke was on me. And there I was. In the headlights like a deer in the forest, head raised, ears pricked, with nowhere to run. Mari got in my face, pressed her small tits against my chest, grabbed my head and held it tightly between her two hands, and planted a wide, sloppy kiss on me. The taste of cigarettes and stale beer, like bad breath, filled my mouth, traveled down my throat to my stomach, and then shot like a speeding bullet straight into my psyche. I shivered. Something carnivorous was after me. She pulled my ear to her mouth and said, "Souza, yur gonna fuck me before the night's over."

There it was! Out in the open. And those assholes just stood there looking at the ground like guilty children.

The rope tightened around my throat. The trapdoor opened, snapping my neck, her words rattling through my brain like a train lurching at high speed. My friends were not my friends. They had conspired against me all along. I had been backed to the edge of the cliff. Fall or fly. Just like the high dive.

I could have just said, "Fuck this. I'm leaving." But I didn't. I was too late. Too many beers, too much off kilter, too much off game. I struggled to dislodge my heart, which had leapt into my throat, stuck there like a big piece of meat. A voice that seemed disconnected to a body but that was, in fact, my voice, in my body, cocky and shaky, said to Mari, "In your dreams, baby, in your dreams." She grinned. She knew she'd won.

"Tonight's my lucky night. My dreams are gonna come true. And that's a fact." There was a note of triumph in her voice, as if she'd just slapped four aces on the table. Her eyes traveled shamelessly up and down the shivering length of my body.

I needed distance. To think. To stall. My throat was dry, my mouth cottony. "I have to take a piss," I said. The darkness into which I stepped was just feet away. Full to bursting, my bladder tore loose and released with an exuberance far removed from how I felt, the rest of me in a kind of paralysis, as if my mind had gone off-line. The ground shifted under me, and I felt as if I were being led blindfolded into obstacles I couldn't even begin to fathom. I heard the river, somber and vague, offering no advice, just rills in creeping water. From the dark space I stood in, I watched the others shifting from foot to foot, shivering, a cold beer can in one hand, the other shoved deep into the pockets, the icy cold having reached the very marrow of our bones.

"Hey, Souza," Craig bleated, "let's get the hell outta here. We're freezin' our nuts off."

Okay, assholes, I thought. "Let's go," I answered, the desperation in my voice missing the mark of the confident, in-charge guy I professed to be. But I was not confident. I was definitely not in charge.

Before we got into the cars, Craig slipped me a small packet with the word "Trojan" printed on it. *Fuck!* I thought and shoved it in my pocket. We got in the cars and left.

The fog had thickened. The hood ornament was barely discernable from behind the wheel. Visibility was near zero, and the cars could do little more than creep. Trent and Mari were sparring back and forth, not making any sense. He was invested in the "big hole, small hole" thing and wouldn't let it go. Mari just laughed, a sound that segued into a cackle and then back to a laugh. It felt like I was driving to my own funeral with two idiot clowns to accompany the body. I was hurt and panicked and drunk. I lashed out at them in my head, too intimidated to speak my mind. I wished spiteful things on them. Trent would get fat, go to the pack; Jerry, good-hearted, unexceptional and prepared, in his life span, to be part of the ordinary business of an ordinary life; Craig—Craig hurt the most. Craig, good-looking, popular, lean, and quick with dreams of being nothing but very rich. Craig, truly capable of treachery. That I'd considered him my best friend was proof of how thin my perception was. How ironic if he should end up very rich—and infertile and childless and alone. Knives in the backs of those whose knives were in me. A useless retaliation. A temporary satisfaction. I'd get over it. Just not right then. And there was still Mari.

———

Mr. Roy's house was several miles away. The perversion of time being what it was, despite our creeping through the fog a few miles per hour, we arrived too soon. A hollow feeling had settled in my stomach. The small bungalow, dark, cold, and waiting, sat there like the cemetery waiting for the cortege. The burial would be inside.

We walked to the front door in tandem, the fog blurring anything two feet away. Droplets of water that had collected on the overhanging branches of a sycamore fell on us like pelting reproaches of rain.

The key pecked to find the hole in my trembling hand as I poked around for the keyhole. I got it in and turned it in the lock, and we filed through the door, me first, feeling along the wall for the light switch. The room seemed to be expecting us, warmed by a wall heater that had been left on and greeted us with nonchalant disarray. The ceiling light, draped in cobwebs, was singled out by the dust that had accumulated on it. And the acrid smell of cat piss burned my nose and made my eyes water, although a cat was nowhere to be seen.

The state of the house was no surprise. Mr. Roy kept house the way he conducted class. Newspapers were strewn about. Piles of dirty dishes were in tippy stacks in the kitchen sink, on the counter, and on various other surfaces. There was a stack of nudie male porn magazines on the floor, slid halfway under the sofa skirt with slices of naked torsos peeking out unselfconsciously. I associated their suggestive, off-color vibe to Mr. Roy's clammy handshake—and Mr. Reeves's from years ago.

"I gotta pee," Mari said and made unsteadily for the bathroom, which adjoined the small living room. The open door introduced the toilet, facing us from the wall with the lid up, as if tipping its hat. She went in and with no compunction, left the door ajar, swaying side to side a little as she did her business.

Maybe she'll just pass out, I thought. Hoped.

The tinkling sound ended and the toilet flushed. Mari came out smiling. "There," she said, "done and ready for bear," giving me a fly-by kiss as she scanned for the bedroom. She didn't have to look far. It was next to the bathroom, its door also wide open.

The four of us weren't sober, but we weren't out-of-control drunk either. The slow drive from the river and the cold air had mellowed the stupor we'd been in, and we were in that dulled, fatigued, in-between state where the alcohol was wearing off. Energy was wearing down. Jerry, Craig, and Trent slouched down on the sofa, legs spread open, taking up more space than was theirs, beers in hand, as if they were an audience for a performance they would be enjoying in their vicarious, grinning, traitoring minds. Mari made her move. Unsteady on her feet but fully in charge, she grabbed me by the hand.

"In here, Studly," she said and led me into the bedroom. I was numb with fear and too riddled with pride to resist. She closed the door behind us to the snickering coming from the living room through thin walls.

I have tried to block out what happened from this point forward. I know I used the rubber. I remember the two of us hurriedly undressing back-to-back, and for a moment in my head I was in Ken's bedroom, a flashback that came and went, absent the intense anticipation of something I'd been waiting for. Before I knew it, I was inside her, my butt muscles tightening with each violent jab, our mouths opening and closing on each other, as if we were trying to be sick. In a few seconds of ignorant thrusting, I jerked and shuddered into her sloppy dark cavern, and it was over. And, as I had hoped, in a few seconds more, she was passed out. Or appeared to be. I slipped out and cautiously stood up, careful not to disturb her. Why risk it? It was bad enough already. And would probably be worse at school. I took the rubber off and threw it into the wastebasket on the floor by the bed.

Mr. Roy would be—what, titillated? Aroused when he found it, *if* he found it? As per our agreement, I was to relate all the details of this debacle, minus the last part, thinking, *The way he keeps house, he might not dump the wastebasket for weeks.* By then, the disgusting thing would be thrown out amid the snotty tissues and candy wrappers.

I hiked my pants up, keeping my eyes on Mari, spread-eagled on the bed, for fear she might wake up and start making comments. On the sagging mattress, a light washed over her from the pink lampshade on the fake crystal lamp on the bedside table, casting a beatific glow over her pearl-white body, sprawled out on mismatched sheets in an incongruous simulation of a Botticelli, spreading her cunt open with two fingers and fiddling with the glistening insides like an unsatisfied child sucking its thumb. The arch of brown hair revealed the truth about her blond hair.

I paused, looking at her. For some reason, it crossed my mind that she was not really the sexual carnivore she made herself out to be, just a little girl who wanted to be loved. Playing with herself, as she was, seemed to be a gesture of despair. What she was giving to herself at that moment was in lieu of a lover who would never come. When she woke up, she'd probably hate me. Although I didn't really care, a brief sense of compassion came over me that was confused with the mix of mortification sticking inside my head about my performance. More than anything, I was still pissed. What if she remembered how bad I was at it? And blabbed about it. So what? Nobody much listened to what she said. I'd claim I was *so* drunk. And I really didn't care what she wanted. Or what she needed. Or even how she would get home. She was only Mari fucking Montrose.

I went back into the living room, not having been gone long enough and not having been loud enough for the three on the sofa to build any smart remarks on. No moans or grunts. A small but solid victory.

Craig said, "Well?"

"Let's go," I snapped. They gaped at me and then at each other and then back at me before they broke up laughing. Craig patted me on the shoulder.

"Nice goin'," he said.

I jerked away to show that no, all was not forgiven. On the other hand, in the few steps it took to get to the door, I knew a small part of my brain had been liberated. I was proud and a bit smug for what I'd done, in spite of how I'd done it, and rested more easily knowing this singular event would stop any rumors floating around school about me. "Let's get the fuck out of here," I said and walked out the door, followed by the others, leaving Mari behind without a second thought. There was suddenly the sensation of merely by leaving the scene, by leaving her behind, we also left their betrayal of me behind as well, the feeling of betrayal mitigated somewhat by my "success." Still, trying to rekindle the camaraderie I'd felt for them before was like trying to light a fire with wet wood. It would take time. We left in separate cars, me in mine, them in the other one, everybody creeping away in the fog.

Christmas came and went. The New Year slipped by, and the nights were once again silent. School started back up. My friendship with Craig, Jerry, and Trent resumed as if nothing had happened. Falling out between friends in high school didn't last. The upside was that my reputation had been elevated. Any whispers about my orientation had been put to rest. Also, Mari's remarks about me stopped. She was clearly no longer creamin' her jeans over me. I was relieved and insulted both.

A few weeks later, I had a girlfriend of my own. We were going steady, my ring around her neck as required. Her name was Nancy Hudson, a nice girl from a nice family, all of whom were delighted with her choice of me as her new, good-looking, popular boyfriend. And the new car and all. She wore my class ring around her neck for two months. I struggled. I counted the days. "I don't want to go steady anymore," I said one night as we sat outside her house in the car with the motor running after what had been a tense, tight-lipped date where I was totally uncommunicative and sullen. In her quivering, parakeet voice and her beautiful, wounded eyes, her face flushed red with a trace of anger and an implicit accusation that I had been deceiving her all along (which, on some level, I had) she turned and looked at me and said flatly, "I thought so." She unfastened the clasp on the chain, sliding the ring off and into my extended hand in one deft gesture, as if she'd been forewarned somehow.

About this time, I'd heard or read somewhere that boys my age pass through a stage of homosexuality, that this is normal, nearly universal. *This might be happening to me,* a part of me thought. Another part thought not, as I remembered Mari naked and spread out on the bed in the Botticelli-like tableau; flash to my performance—on her, in her. The effect on me lingered, like the side effect of a strong medicine. I didn't see myself going down that road again, and decided Nancy deserved someone more inclined to commit to an honest boy-girl relationship than I was going to offer. She had no idea what was going on in my head when I was with her. Or trying to be with her. Even so, as I walked her to the car one sunny winter afternoon in January 1957 with my ring around her neck and my arm around her waist, I thought I might get married someday. The very next day I asked for my ring back wondering, *What happens to people like me?* Dudley Igo gave me the answer the following year.

CHAPTER 8

DUDLEY IGO'S ENGLISH CLASS

THERE ARE CERTAIN INDIVIDUALS who walk among the general population unnoticed, too discreet in their manner to draw attention to themselves. Even so, when they enter a room, you know at a glance they're smart. Mr. Dudley Igo was one of those people. But he never flaunted his intelligence. He didn't need to. It emanated. He was the kind of smart person my father said would never make any money. Mr. Igo was a classic intellectual. The real deal. He was also the teacher for senior English.

There was a new eraser on each desk the first day of class. It was one of Mr. Igo's subtle lessons in life, although we didn't understand the meaning that first day. It represented something we'd need for our senior essays, as well as our mistake-filled adult lives. On the last day of class, another new eraser was on each desk, and he explained it this way: "You've used the old one on your assignments; now use this one in your lives." Even his humor was instructive.

Besides his grasp of the written word, he could discuss films and film directors, past and present, as deftly as he could writers and literature—quick references that were relevant to the main subject. Questions posed by the class took on heightened tones; they were thoughtful, inquisitive, and more serious than in other classes. We stretched to express ourselves in bigger and brighter polysyllabic words, trying to impress him, to garner favor, a ploy he never fell for. He was too far ahead of us.

His reading assignments were varied but veered toward period pieces. The *rococo* and the *baroque*. He said, "The baroque is more muscular, the rococo is lighter and more decorative," adding, "The rococo is the final deliquescence of the baroque," as if we had any idea what *deliquescence* meant. "Very Heathcliffean," we heard before we'd been assigned *Wuthering Heights*. References like these came and went, speeding by like hummingbirds, tossed off as sparks of literary clarity. "Try to look at things from Shakespeare's point of view," he suggested as we plodded through *Macbeth*. "How it was in the seventeenth century. Disruption was everywhere—in nature as well as in the royal house." Then he'd link comparisons, then to now, deftly, quickly, making old words seem new, not shying away from his own personal opinions. "In every line, there is evidence of richness that makes him the greatest writer of all time." Bold declarations delivered with angular earnestness.

At six feet four, his stature among the other teachers was literal as well as figurative, and he stood in stark contrast to the rest of the faculty, some of whom had been there for generations teaching under the umbrella of tenure. He was like the Great Library of Alexandria, a colossal structure among ordinary buildings, driven by a sophisticated code, the standard of which was so elevated that no other teacher knew what the code was, let alone have the ability to teach by it. He prepared his classes for college-level work and conducted them as if senior students were already at university. He also cut no slack. A good grade from Mr. Igo was like winning the lottery, except it was due to hard work not luck.

His contrast to the rest of the faculty was sharp, even though, as I now reimagine some of them, ones we mocked or made fun of, I am less critical, affectionate, even, recognizing they, too, were the stuff of rich material, as rich as characters from a Tennessee Williams play—ordinary, extraordinary folks leading ordinary, extraordinary lives. Or outrageous ones. From my perspective now, it's easy to imagine some of my teachers in the back row of the State Theater, not the Del Rio. Or lying next to one another on Lover's Island at Marysville's Ellis Lake instead of dancing at the Moon Lake Casino where Blanche DuBois's lover took his own life with a bullet to the head. Or ensconced in the Davis Hotel in Marysville's red-light district—its own incarnation of Williams's Tarantula Arms.

Their names and faces come back with very little effort. I can never forget diaphanous Miss Dunlap, dumpy and powdered white, glowing eerily like Baudelaire's swan, perfumed with essence of lilac, loose wisps of hair a distraction from her Latin conjugations, and as befuddled as Marion Lorne, insisting we learn, and even sing, "Guadeamus igitur, juvenes dum sumus," and when she was feeling theatrical, singing along with us in a high, thin, quivery voice, flushing with feigned embarrassment at her own performance.

In contrast to her was fierce, stork-like Miss Fillmore, at five foot one, all sharp angles and cubistic face, long, thin, and triangular like a skinny cat's, screeching the principles of mechanical drawing from my father's class up through the years to mine, standing all day straight as a dart—rigid, in fact.

Mr. Henry, built like a sack of something thick and unhealthy, his head joined directly to his body as if a neck was inconsequential, his speech a replication of Elmer Fudd's and who, against all odds, made history more boring than it already was as he paced back and forth in his cheap shoes at the front of the class with his hands clasped behind his back. Staying awake in his class was a challenge we met by passing notes as he droned on with the blob of gravy or Bolognese from cafeteria lunchtime on a terrible tie or a stain of unidentifiable origin on the front of his shiny suit pants.

There was slight Mr. Seimas, short and strangely erect, almost paralytic with tension, teaching French like a terrier gone to ground, with panicked green eyes that he squeezed shut as if confined to a trap of his own making, the scant strands of oily hair slickly plastered across his small head.

I remember, too, the girls' PE coach, Miss Brooks, whom I observed from a distance, since girls' PE was, well, girls' PE. "Brooksie" dressed in gym shorts and a man's white gaucho shirt, a whistle around her neck and her naturally wavy hair cut like a man's, parted on one side but slightly longer as if to suggest she was less masculine than she was. She was athletic and full of energy, as her vocation would suggest, with a quick smile that had uneven curves in it due to an asymmetrical scar that cut deeply down one cheek, causing the eye on that side to be constricted almost into a squint.

Miss Frohman, dean of girls, was always dressed in two-piece gabardine suits with kick-pleated skirts, not pants, which now I think she would have rather worn, in one of three colors—brown, dark green, or maroon—and a white nylon blouse buttoned at the neck so unfrivolous that it suggested the absence of a man's tie. No jewelry, a little lipstick strictly for appearances, and high-heeled shoes that were clunky, not high at all, low enough to not even suggest high. She probably would have been pretty in her youth, her pleasant features indicating as much. Now, rather handsome. At five feet with imposing carriage that belied her height, and being detached and diplomatic, she appeared taller than she was. She was handsome, unfeminine.

There is no doubt in my mind that both she and Brooksie were lesbians, an assumption I draw from years of exposure to various lifestyles. In the 1950s, lesbianism was a subject that was handled with almost invisible discretion. The word "lesbian" was foreign and existed like a foreign country until, a decade later, Gertrude Stein and Alice B. Toklas entered my frame of reference. I can't remember hearing the word in high school much, if at all.

There was subversively fey, handsome Mr. Bond, who had a network of small broken veins catacombing his nose like a microscopic map of nowhere—the sign of a solitary drinker, I think. He was a polite, considerably extroverted man, friendly but not offensively so, but seemed burdened, now that I am into armchair psychoanalysis, by a nagging frustration that showed in a constantly furrowing brow. There were also clues I picked up on during his typing class. I studied him while he stood at a preferred place at the second-floor window while we typed, very keen on the runners from gym class coming in from the field at the end of laps, breathless, sunlit torsos glistening with sweat like revelations. Sitting behind him in the cacophony of clacking Underwoods, trying for fifty mistake-free words a minute, I often wondered what he was thinking as he stared out the window at these athletes. And me being me, I invented possibilities both erotic and titillating.

In an overview of the teachers and faculty as a whole, you would have to say that the world of style and fashion had left them behind. Nevertheless, no one, least of all me, would deny there was an art to what they did in instilling knowledge and aspiration in varying degrees to their charges, just as there is an art to everything. Like Picasso, some painted with creativity and passion, like Mr. Igo. Some painted with their fingers. Like children.

And then, of course, in his Quonset hut at a far remove from the rest, was Mr. Roy, the most Tennessee Williams–like of all.

———

Unlike other classrooms where the doors were left open from first bell to last, as if that would clear the air of student torpor, Mr. Igo's door was locked until he arrived, implying that within the room there was something of great value and, by being locked, the escape of special information was prevented. We gathered at the door early one by one, being late never a consideration. He came rushing through us, apologizing, "Excuse me. Pardon," as if he, himself, were late, which he never was, fishing the key from his pocket with one hand and balancing an armload of books and papers in the other arm. We filed in behind him. The bell rang. The door closed. We took our seats. Class began.

He was in a hurry to get started. He was always in a hurry—in a hurry to get from point A to point B and in a hurry to educate, as if time were running out and there was no way to teach us all he wanted to, all we needed to know.

I was a straight-A, confident, blasé student, but, intimidated by his reputation, I took a seat in the middle of the room instead of at the front, as in other classes. I sat very upright with my hands clasped on the textbook in the center of the desk and my ankles crossed underneath, as if symmetry might make me less conspicuous. The smartest of the senior class were a little nervous in the beginning, including the class valedictorian, Kyoko Watanabe.

We waited for Mr. Igo like an audience waits for the curtain to rise. He laid the armful of papers in rough stacks on the desk, closed his eyes for a moment like a brief meditation, and then began.

"All right, class, today we're going to be reading Walt Whitman," he declared as a fait accompli. Everyone straightened up and pulled themselves to attention. He coughed, dryly, briefly, the first words quivering, excited about what he was saying. And so, to Whitman we went.

Mr. Igo began by explaining how many times the poet had written and rewritten *Leaves of Grass* and why, and as I listened, I found myself comparing his, Mr. Igo's, eloquence to his diametrically opposing appearance. Like Ichabod Crane, he was a gangly form, all arms and legs, wearing oversized tortoiseshell glasses that sat crookedly on his longish, noble nose, an appendage that veered neither right nor left and still suggested an element of doubt, as if he might at any moment question himself. His wardrobe was as autumnal as his mildly wild hair, combed in a rush before putting on a rumpled, tweedy jacket that matched the rumpled tweed of his hair. His ties were nubby and knitted and his shoes, brogues, size 13, were highly polished over deep scuff marks. His clothes exuded the dry essence of pencil shaving and chalk dust—the smell of classrooms—in the same way the hallways smelled of floor wax and the lavatories of Pine-Sol.

His eyes, hazel and timid, moved constantly as he spoke or as he listened. And his boyish face, badly pockmarked from his own teenage years, lent an indistinct connection of him to his students, with an inside track on youth, and established a comfort zone between him and his class that couldn't exist with other teachers. He appeared to notice nothing around him, but he saw or sensed everything. While writing on the blackboard with his back to the class, he could anticipate questions about what he had written before they were asked. You could never catch him off guard. He was always one step ahead.

His command of the room was absolute, achieved not by duress but through the intellectual integrity he brought with him every day. And as a result, unruly or inappropriate behavior was nonexistent. Students asked questions earnestly. He answered with equal earnestness, quick to correct or clarify using his fine, patrician hands as a conductor uses a baton, his nuanced expression holding a reserve of additional knowledge.

How he looked and how he acted, however, does not convey the largesse of what he gave us. He was a leader who never led a parade or fought for a cause except the cause of erudition. This made him far more than the sum of his parts and beautiful in a way that went beyond physical description. His effect on our—on my—education was like a big exclamation mark at the end of a long sentence. He promised much and delivered much more, and he shed a light on a part of me I had not been able to find. For this I am eternally grateful.

I struggled with most of what we had been assigned and struggled even more when we had to write about it, just as I am struggling now. When I tried to put my thoughts into words, what was clear and sharp in my mind was tangled and clumsy when I wrote it down, not so different from what I'm doing here. *Moby Dick*, *Ulysses*, Tennyson. Formidable and over my head. What were they talking about? And Proust's languished descriptions going on and on for pages: "Love . . ., ever unsatisfied, lives always in the moment that is about to come." What did that mean exactly? Emerson's philosophy of transcendentalism contradicted the Christian doctrine I'd been spoon-fed by the Nazarenes, even though by the time I entered high school, what I had learned from the fundamentalists was a good lesson in what not, and how not, to believe. Disavow your own destiny? Like who you are is in disagreement with who they say you should be? So, Emerson resonated. I related to the premise that we trust ourselves on what's right, that our intuitive knowledge goes beyond the senses. This was reasonable. Christianity had laid sin at the feet of these same senses—sex, dancing, lipstick even, and brought God's wrath upon humanity. But intuition rather than guilt? Good thinking. I carried guilt around like a sack of rocks, and I was tired of it.

Apart from the classics we were assigned, one best-selling novel struck a chord: *Raintree County*. I identified with its secrets and strange love, and in time would send it to Jack as a cryptic reminder from an anonymous source of what we could have had but had lost. The language, which I could easily understand, as well as the glamorous, romantic visuals, were transposed into a movie of the same name starring Elizabeth Taylor and Montgomery Clift, bringing the story to life in the way a book couldn't, depicting the unfulfilled quest for love, a notion I had grappled with, and which was, I thought then, an appropriate if melodramatic representation of Jack and me. Additionally, a real-life drama followed on the heels of the publication and was an element of notoriety that surrounded the book's release. The author,

Ross Lockridge Jr., had committed suicide after he finished writing it. Tragedy that was right up my alley.

Thomas Mann's *Death in Venice* drew me inside the obsessive, repressed desire of Professor Aschenbach for the beautiful, the unattainable Tadzio and how it destroyed Aschenbach. I couldn't help but draw parallels. Although there was no age difference between Jack and me, as there is in Mann's novella, there was a great emotional distance, existing, I have concluded, because of my early sexual history with Bobby Reeves and the grown-up nature of our affair. Aschenbach had lost his wife. Bobby left me, which, at the early impressionable age I was then, felt like a death. Several years later, I was still grieving for him in some way. Aschenbach repressed his libidinal drives. So did I. There was nothing but silence between Aschenbach and Tadzio. The silence in my family culture with regard to personal feelings was a way of life. So the distances and limited conversation between Jack and me were familiar. And in his own way, Jack was elusive, like Tadzio, and represented beauty and a concept of love that was unattainable.

"Throbbing between two lives," from T. S. Eliot's *The Waste Land* hit home. A tormented soul throbbing melodramatically between two lives was me. But Walt Whitman, mystifying on one level, clear as a bell on the another, peeled with clarity that touched my soul.

The Whitman assignment came at us almost as a dare, so full of energy, like a flag whipping to start a race. I remember I was not feeling up to the challenge of what was sure to be obtuse poetry and felt as though I could retreat into a state of mind I called "temporary fadeout," a daydreaming drift to things more provocative than poetry. It was a peculiar but effective device of my own invention. I could take it anywhere—school gossip, sexual fantasy, a recent movie, or anything that would take me away from where I was. It could come in fragments or abstractions full of sexual imagery and lust or as an unattainable scenario that would come apart like paper in water. I could construct a fiction that extended a casual encounter to a prolonged, complicated affair. A second or the full hour. And undetectable. It often revolved around Jack, then three years in the past—a lifetime ago—but bringing him back with a force that produced a sting. I could imagine him reaching across the sheets for me, the double curve of his back sweeping from spine to buttock like the architectural beauty of a harp striking the note of a love song that had changed from a minor key to a major one. (My imagination could be over the top.) Or to Bobby, even though his image had started to blur. If I thought of him too obsessively or with projections of what might have been, so divorced from reality that it could have never come to pass, my heart could clench in an excitement more sexual than if I were with him in the flesh. Or Harold, even, and the orgasms he brought me to and about which I've yet to write. I might simply repeat what I'd constructed some time before, maybe fantasies, whose existences were as real to me as they were invisible to everyone else. My proclivity to construct pockets of imagined time, projections coming from and going to nowhere, served me in the moment. My inclination to indulge in temporary fadeout was strong. I had to be careful.

Whitman described feelings that were melancholic, easy to feel and understand. He wrote of sensations felt along the heart rather than in the heart, a thread that built into an emotional rollercoaster. His language described inexpressible feelings I had. His words became my obsession. I wanted more. His hand had extended an invitation into the mystery and wonder of the human heart. I needed to go there.

The other great works of literature were not able to do for me what Whitman did. He wrote about what went before and just how far there was to go. He was the extra step, a push to a quantum leap. The more I read, the more the words ignited a series of confrontations in the labyrinth of my confused and whirling mind, a maze that also became a mirror. It was all there. Words clarified feelings that spoke to past experience—Bobby, Jack, the mindless sex with myself— the abominable sin "self-abuse." The past, present, and maybe even a fleeting glimpse into the future were made clearer. And the way he mocked religion while proclaiming the world holy couldn't have made more sense to me.

I was no longer on the outside of myself looking in. I saw myself as I was—different and yet the same. I could accept that. Whitman clarified what some private part of me had believed all along—the conviction that society was wrong, not me. I could reject not only the notion that my sexual nature was abhorrent but desire itself was part of a universal consciousness. *We* became *one*. One heart, one mind, one body. From the opening lines of *Song of Myself*, I understood what I had experienced with Jack, if only momentarily.

I celebrate myself,

And what I shall assume you shall assume,

For every atom belonging to me as good belongs to you.

Mr. Igo had no inkling about my revelations. There was no reason why he would. And he could never have realized the impact the assignment had on me. But that he understood the full meaning of the writer's work, there is no doubt. The taboo substance, still illegal, was left to the imagination of those reading between the lines. Mr. Igo's focus was on the boundaries Whitman had broken from traditional themes to the mystical aspects of life in all its physicality, which, in his hand, became new and larger. Words were treated as tangible, tactile objects and suggested that on some higher plane, language and the human body were equals. The hymn-like cadence of the writing was familiar, not unlike the rhythm of Bible verse, but at a far remove from the biblical mumbo-jumbo. It was music I could understand. God is the blue sky. God is man. God is leaves of grass.

"Think motive and metaphor," Mr. Igo said, "and subtext." Aha! There it was! Subtext. Something I could sink my teeth into, wrap my head around. *Tea and Sympathy. Rebel Without a Cause*, the subtexts in the themes were more seeable by then. Hollywood bent its rigid moral code, if only a little. Messages were there if you were keen enough, even if the characters were, and still mostly are, depicted as troubled or tragic. In the decades that followed, barriers were taken down, but slowly. *Boys in the Band* broke ground Off Broadway, moved to Broadway, and became a major motion picture in 1970. But the theme was just an expanded, elaborate spectacle of a group of unhappy, troubled, men living unhappy, troubled lives. Even so, when projected onto the big screen where images are truly larger than life, it was clear that text had grown wings. Gay men were still conflicted, self-deprecating, but the story gave a certain emotional honesty, and therefore a beauty, to them as individuals. They were drawn in more than one dimension even though still portrayed as tragic. It was a compensation. It was also a step in the right direction. In 1973, the American Psychiatric Association took homosexuality off its list of character disorders and neuroses. It was from then on considered within the normal range of sexual behavior. However, the stigma lingered and, to a degree, still does.

In *Leaves of Grass* and *I Sing the Body Electric*, Whitman found beauty as he saw it every day. Passages jumped out. He wrote what he lived, despite the fact that it was criminalized in its time and was a crime a hundred years later. In 1957, he was still considered socially and morally dicey, even as we read him.

A man's emotions for another man and the intricate pleasure it proposed were heinous notions, abhorrent to Western civilization's puritanical belief. Body and spirit must be held as separate entities. Physical pleasure was a moral issue, a moral guilt. Whitman made it simple: the body was nature; the body was God.

"Other words wanted . . ." I knew what he meant. "I feel a hundred realities clearly determined in me that words are not yet formed to represent . . ." I knew what he meant. Language had caught up with experience. "As I walk by your side or sit near, or remain in the same room with you, little you know the subtle electric fire that for your sake is playing within me." "Dismiss whatever insults your own soul." Everything he said rang true. And magical. I heard my own voice in them, coming from some deeper place, echoing from the center of me. A manner of being. *Love not only the world. Love yourself as well.* That's what I heard. I had found what I was meant to find.

"Hot wishes." "Love flag." "Love-flesh swelling and deliciously aching." Phrases that rocketed straight into my heart and burst, the words descending as stars; tactile images climbed hand over hand up the length of my body and entered my brain; erotic stirrings curled and straightened. "Sometimes you just have to hold back." I rejected this. I finally knew why. I took my first step away from any need to confess who I was or to justify myself in the eyes of others. A new belief, an acceptance of self, had me soaring upward into a beautiful place, speculative, dangerous, perhaps, as if I were streaking naked in the night air or feeling the thrill of a flying, falling swan dive. I was in a new dimension, a metropolis of bustling possibility from the remote suburb of me. What I thought could never be mine and was out of reach might now be not only a right but an inevitability. There was a parade outside. It was calling me. I knew I could join it, no longer hanging back in the crowd. I knew and I understood. I understood the erection in the shallow end of the pool. I understood what Bobby had shown me. I understood the aching in the dark with Jack. I recognized my rite of spring. Sometimes in life, you have a moment of pure clarity. This was one of those moments. I had come face-to-face with myself and the great exhilaration of rightness. Words took me out of this world and back into it. They resided in me like permanent habitations.

Mr. Igo read passages aloud in front of the class, his voice paper-fine and clear. Some of the passages struck with so much force that I committed them to memory: "Through me forbidden voices/Voices of sexes and lusts, voices veiled and I remove the veil,/Voices indecent by me clarified and transfigured."

CHAPTER 9

THE CLASS REUNION

High School Graduation, 1958.

P AST AND PRESENT COME FACE-TO-FACE at high school class reunions. They stand toe-to-toe, staring each other down. I couldn't help but wonder how two such different times would stack up against each other at the reunion I was on my way to. I had avoided going to any of the others until this one—the twenty-fifth. But this one seemed infinitely more significant. It had been a quarter of a century. It was the summer of 1983.

I'm not sure what I expected. A grand revelation, perhaps. But, as we learn, revelations work on their own timeline, not ours. As significant as a quarter-century event might be, I seriously doubted it would rise to the nostalgic magnitude of feeling I would have hoped for. And, at age forty-two, I was still capable of absurd expectations, even though I knew better. Unsurprisingly, the event turned out to be very different than I anticipated. Vodka martinis dragged up regrets and old wounds, both of which, like desire, needed satisfaction, and I was able to subvert the social into the sexual. I'd had a bad feeling the minute I'd dropped the reservation in the mail. I should have listened to my intuition.

How do I look? I asked myself, checking the slice of face in the rear-view mirror. How would *they* look? Better than me? Not as good? I missed the turn into the country club.

I hadn't been to the Peach Tree since I left home for college. I remembered that the food was too expensive and not particularly good. The Peach Tree Golf and Country Club was the only private club in the greater twin cities then, the only game in town where, after you'd paid the twenty-five-hundred-dollar initial membership fee, a big sum in the 1950s when it was built, and fifty-dollar dues every month, you could go anytime, pay more for green fees and mixed drinks than anywhere else in town, and rub elbows with the who's-who-in-the-zoo. It was an amicable mix of old and new money, classes mixing and cocktails blurring social lines.

My father had several ways to smile, depending on what he was smiling about. His mouth would configure itself in different ways. When he came home and announced he had joined the country club, the particular turn of his lips told me the smile he wore was the proud one. We were not of old money—the Gold Rush rich—but modestly of the new. Starting with nothing but a strong work ethic, my family had, in two words, *made it.*

Since graduation, I had been out of touch with almost everyone in my class. I wondered how, or if, we would relate to one another. I had left the house with good intentions, thinking I'd reinvigorate old relationships, ones I'd been fond of but lost contact with, and curious about what the overall high school class looked like after twenty-five years—how they'd held up, or how they'd been let down; which ones had sailed into the calm waters of family life and simply vanished within their own marriages. We had all left school as all young people do, certain of what will make us happy. Until we find out that wasn't it.

And I also wanted to find out what had happened to Johnathan Pierce Swift. What had happened to him? Where had the arc of life had taken him after he left and I thought I couldn't go on? Even though you always do. I'd gotten over him when it mattered a great deal more than it did now, when it had been an almost unbearable loss and I had long since resigned myself to the fact that I'd probably never see him again. But I'd finally be able to admit the lesson I'd learned about myself: my capacity to not see the truth when it was directly in my face was staggering. Nevertheless, there was still an open wound somewhere in my heart. I was sure the blistering memory would be revisited in some way at this milestone event even though I had a hunch he wouldn't be there. I nearly turned around and went home.

For all I knew, he could be dead. I wondered if I could hold a grudge against a dead person. He had almost become an abstraction, but the thought of him still had a strange power over me, not through any conscious exertion of his will—he had held no place in my life—but because, I realized, my permission for this was willingly given. He is alive to me only in these words on paper.

I've had a recurring dream over the years that won't break, as a fever eventually does. Sometimes a dream is just a dream, like the song says. But sometimes it's more than a dream. This one always felt like more than a dream. In it, I am on a train pulling away from the platform. Jack is standing, watching me leave. The train gains speed and as I look back from the window, he gets smaller and smaller until he disappears. I wake up. My chest is tight like a fist. I have tried to trivialize him out of existence but can't. He is what Henry James called "the tragic part of happiness." Small things bring him back—piano notes in a smoky bar or a smeared reflection in a window. I remember him in detail, as Proust would, on page after page. I wonder if he ever thinks of me. Could memory occupy as much of his time as it does mine?

As I got closer to the country club, memories also got closer, not farther, even as time continued to move things away. I parked some distance from the other cars and sat watching couples getting out of theirs, fluffing and slicking their hair, checking makeup, straightening ties, arm in arm, other couples following in similar preparations. As I watched, I knew I didn't love my friends as I used to. So cynical. I was like a Sam Sheppard character, observing others and skeptical of myself.

I followed far enough behind so I didn't need to interact. I wasn't ready. I dreaded the demands of polite exchanges, not sure I could hold up to surface conversation so distant from the more profound thoughts beneath it. I paused and glanced at the slivered moon and the remote stars, wondering if their murky presence was an omen. Omens aren't real, I know. But I thought of them as if they were or could be. It's a quirk of mine.

Small talk, the Vaseline of social intercourse, lay just behind the carved double doors—lots of "Remember when we . . ." trying to resurrect bonhomie of years ago. Cocktails would reignite the bonding of youth. Maybe.

Events like these are not my forte. I am anxious, insecure, and prone to snap judgments. My tolerance for feigned interest wears thin quickly. Something I'm not proud of. Liquor brings out my dark side. Something else I'm not proud of. With the voices in my head, the caged monkeys, always alive and waiting, I had to be particularly careful if I was going to get what I wanted.

As much as I dwell in the past, or the past dwells in me, I am not very good at talking about it, particularly with people I haven't seen for years and to whom I wasn't close to begin with. Conversation becomes a kind of charade. I hold up my side of the bargain with questions about families and jobs, nodding, staring thoughtfully at their faces while I'm in and out of temporary fadeout, the trick I still use. I'll excuse myself with, "Getting another drink. Be right back. Get one for you?" And, as I walk away, I hear murmurings about what a good conversationalist I am, when "Oh, really?" or "How nice for you," has been the extent of my contribution. "We should have him over for dinner sometime."

I swiped my hands down each side of my hips to wipe the moisture from my palms, and as I reached for the door, old emotions arose as fog does between the trees, blanketing the landscape like white tempera. The romantic part of me comes back in a flash with the length of my body pressed against his backside. I entered the foyer to the sound of music from the '50s, perfect for the occasion.

I was checked off a list by a woman sitting at a long table where rows of photo badges were lined up in alphabetical order. From the big spaces on the table, I surmised that almost everyone who was coming was already here. My senior class photo stared up at me from its isolated spot. Another omen.

As I pinned on the badge, I glanced around at other badges standing near enough to see. They bore little likeness to those on whom they were pinned, a quick and typically uncharitable appraisal. The men were bald or on their way; the women plumpish or dowdy or on their way to either or both. And as I scanned the large Caucasian crowd, I thought probably everyone there was a Republican. It was likely. California valley towns were, and still are, mostly red.

"Wait a minute," my ex-classmate, the girl (I should be calling her *lady?*) tending the reception table said, staring thoughtfully at me. After a pause that robbed her of credence, she said, "Oh, yeah. I remember you." Clearly, she didn't. That was okay. I didn't remember her either. The badges were going to come in handy.

The main room was crowded but not as crowded as the bar. White polyester-draped tables stood on the perimeter of the dance floor. The packed, no-host bar was to one side. *"I'm all dressed up for the dance,"* Marty Robbins sang, hard to hear over the uninterpretable mingling of voices. But the lyrics to "A White Sports Coat and a Pink

Carnation" were clear enough that I could have sung along had I wanted. It felt like I'd stepped into an after-the-game dance. Hearing Marty was like not having grown old. For a minute.

But were these really my classmates? Or their parents? Thinning hair, bulging middles, and clothes that were inconsistent with '50s music threw me for a second. Then I started to identify couples from the way they moved on the dance floor: smooth, coordinated, clumsy, in time with the music, or not. Just like in school. No. I was in the right place.

A man several sheets to the wind grabbed me from behind by the elbow. "Hey! Richie!" (Nobody called me *Richie* anymore. It was *Richard* and had been since college.) "How ya doin' anyway?" Before I could respond, he continued, "Remember all those great times we had?" I remembered neither the "great times" nor this guy, beet-faced and backslapping, with his face way to close for comfort, so close I thought a kiss might be forthcoming. I squinted. Did I remember him? I tried to reconfigure what was in front of me with a full head of hair and fifty pounds less. The photo and name on his badge didn't jog my memory.

"Meeting some people. Catch ya later," I said over my shoulder as I pulled away, his tight grip having left a wrinkle on my linen sleeve. I caught a glimpse of an old girlfriend standing arm-in-arm with a man I assumed was her husband. They were far and away the most glamorous couple in the crowd. He was tanned and slightly graying at the temple, and she—Betty was her name—was completely stunning in a black chiffon over-one-shoulder cocktail dress, wearing no jewelry, which gave terrific impact to the very large solitaire diamond ring on her wedding finger. The cut of the dress was simplicity itself, the kind that screams taste and restraint, qualities that were a big departure from her high school reputation. She was very popular and had been fairly free with her favors then. Or so it was rumored. I overheard a comment in passing that didn't surprise me. "If Betty shows up, you can bet she'll look sensational." She did. And I needed to avoid her. The history there, hers and mine, intermingled with my history with Jack.

Even though we all were on the other side of forty, some of us had aged pretty well. I put myself in that category. I'm allowed. It's my book. I was forty-two to be exact. Looked younger physically, felt older temperamentally, in that my cynicism was running higher with every trip to the bar. That said, I *was* in good shape. I did free weights, used the machines, the Stairmaster. I ran. I was, and am, the quintessential gym rat. A *lifer*, in gym-speak—someone who has taken care of themselves over the long haul. (In my sixties, I would stop running—knee issues—forgo the weights, the machines, the Zumba classes, and all the other stuff for the heady and more gentle practice of yoga.)

At the right distance and in the right light, some of both sexes looked good, almost as good as they did in school. Everything looks better after a few vodka martinis.

A woman I vaguely remembered, stout and caustic-looking now, stopped on her way someplace else, clearly in her cups and appearing to be more or less wandering about on her own. She declared to no one in particular that she was on husband number two or three, she couldn't remember which, after which she laughed with her head thrown back, the contents of her very full glass swishing over the top, down the sides, and down her hand. "And," she added, "I'm getting bored all over again," becoming serious for a moment. She moved on, chuckling to herself.

Monterey Beach, circa 1983.

I bought a drink. "Make it a double," I said to the bartender and proceeded to shuffle through the crowd trying to find a decent fit. "Hi. How are ya? Good. You? Good." Not immediately finding the right niche. Clichés flew by right and left as I moved from one spot to another. "Boy, ever think we'd be this old?" "Time flies when you're havin' fun." "One thing's for sure, it's not like it used to be." "Yeah, yeah, yeah. I like marriage too. But you have to admit life doesn't really get started until the fireworks end."

I moved under the low cloud of cigarette smoke that hovered over the room in stratified layers. The idea of a smoke-filled room seems so strange now. As I threaded my way through the crowd, I imagined I was getting the same kind of scrutiny the coach and Bobby got at the pool that day. *Is my deviance showing?* Paranoia started creeping in. *You're judging me? Really? You might ask yourselves, how many husbands in the room are getting blow jobs in the river bottoms and how many wives are getting serviced by the young stud cutting the lawn every Tuesday who fucks them in a terrifically frightening way? Nothing like the husband, I'll bet.* I was only on my second double. Cocktails were taking me in the direction of maudlin self-pity.

The forty-somethings on the dance floor were getting creepier by the minute, like watching high-stepping ghosts out for a night on the town, some men still wearing bellbottoms popular in the 1960s and '70s and swinging thick-armed wives around. "And with no other choice, we do turn our handsome youth over to life," a quote that came out of nowhere, as quotes have a habit of doing with me. I headed to the bar, three-deep by then.

I elbowed through; pushy behavior didn't seem rude at this point. People had not yet felt that herd inclination of shifting *en masse* toward the dining tables, where, once seated, the gray prime rib or tepid chicken cordon bleu, depending on what box you checked when you RSVP'd with your check (fifty dollars if single, one hundred a couple) would come sailing through the swinging kitchen doors on large round trays high over the heads of the waiters and distributed to either the beef people or the chicken people.

I continued to mill around, stopped here and there to exchange greetings and hugs, cheek kissing with ex-close friends who were eager to share pictures of the kids, flipping photos in my face, the plastic-sleeved accordion albums in their wallets aching to unfold. The subject of family and kids was wearing thin, the spit bucket increasingly heavy. I could feel the small muscles around my mouth and eyes contract in the courteous ritual of forced smiles. I fixed my eyes on the mouth of the person talking, watching the changing shapes of the lips and tongue, the distraction obliterating every word they said—a time-honored trick that always worked. All the time, I'm thinking, *I live in the past so much more than other men do. More like a woman.*

Finding out about Jack seemed more and more remote. Who might know something? But, as much as I craved to see him, talk to him even, to see what he looked like now, I was also slightly relieved. The reality might have been more shock than I could bear.

I pushed my way back to the bar and ended up standing next to a big blonde I seemed to remember as smaller. "How've you been after all these years?" I said with enthusiasm I had to stretch to reach.

"Great," she enthused back.

Against my better judgment, aided by the boldness of alcohol, I blurted, "Say, I just thought of something. Remember that guy, Jack, who was in our class?"

"Jack who?"

"You know, Jack. Messy. Left-handed. Kept to himself. Sexy in a James Dean kind of way. Wonder what ever happened to him."

She frowned a bit, seeing through my pretense (unless I was just imagining it). "Um, don't really know. Excuse me," and she turned, pushing her way from the bar and disappearing in the crowd. Oh well.

I allowed myself another minute at the bar before circulating again. More drinks. More flashbacks. That's how this was going to go. I wasn't giving up. I'd continue to investigate, for whatever good it would do. Still—why, exactly? What was in it for me, really? Closure, perhaps? Weren't Jack and I "closed" after my one ill-timed, misplaced overture? Was nostalgia simply nostalgia? Curiosity just curiosity? That inbred Portuguese tendency toward melancholia? I had no answers. And booze was only exacerbating the issue. I knew that.

I moved from group to group in steps that clearly indicated I should no longer go to the bar. And the thought wasn't lost on me that each gathering I drifted into and out of, I had opened the door for comments and/or conclusions about me, once I was out of earshot. I was the only person there unattached, as it were; no one on my arm. Questions about my status as a single person went unasked in my presence, almost as if they knew. But when I left? An unmarried guy in his forties? Really?

I knew the shift that was coming all too well. Threads of melancholia warmed my blood and crept into my mood. My perspective shifted again; judgments came fast and with little mercy. That Portuguese thing burst forth, its presence as clear as my dark eyes and greasy skin. I had to watch it. Congeniality gone south, turning me into something sharp and teary. I had had just about enough of the John Updike, mid-century, middle-class life, and it was starting to show.

Clear images got fuzzy; four faces became eight and then four again. My head was a hodge-podge of disparate things: Bobby as Superman, the sound of his stockinged feet down the hall; Jack's birthmark; calling to my mother from the bathroom, "Mommy, I'm done." I had been served the fatal cocktail—the one that turns me from borderline profound to blithering idiot when I could no longer tell whether I was being rude or charming or if what I was saying was the opposite of what I meant.

"Whatever happened to Jack . . . what's his name . . . Swift?" I blurted out to no one in particular, almost as if I were talking to myself, a slug of double vodka martini on the rocks forming the words for me and giving me a who-gives-a-fuck-at-this-point-anyway attitude. I stared into my drink as if the answer were at the bottom of the glass as the question repeated itself in my head. "Whatever happened to Jack? Whatever happened to Jack?" People looked at each other and shrugged, not interested in the question much less the answer, as they searched for an escape from dreary, drunk me.

Except for one couple. They shared a look when I mentioned his name, like they knew something and were going to keep quiet. I wasn't so far gone not to notice that. I realized the woman had been a good friend of Jack's cheerleader girlfriend. What did they know? Then they spoke up.

"Fried his brain on drugs after college, I think," the man said. "Don't know for sure." "Had an accident on the farm," I heard. "Tractor rolled on him." "Lucky to be alive, I guess," added the woman. "Has to wear a colostomy bag now. But I know he didn't marry Judy. They split up after a big fight. Something about holding back, or something, she told me."

The impact of a two-by-four between the eyes would have been less severe. I was the son of the son of a farmer. I knew all about heavy equipment. And what can happen when a foot or hand slips off a pedal or a gear. I could see him pinned under a tractor, blood pooling under him. Tears welled up.

"I need some air," I said and made my way through the slider to the outside deck. Frankie Lymon and The Teenagers were singing, *"Why do birds sing so gay, and lovers await the break of day? Why do they fall in love?"* Clutching the wet glass of the sixth or seventh cocktail through a wet, disintegrating napkin, I leaned over and vomited cheese sticks and crudité into the bed of pink azaleas.

The outside shadows were a welcoming respite, a stark contrast to the near neon of the room inside. I entered the darkness easily, standing in the sobering night air and looking back through the slider into a brightly lit room, luxuriating in the wreckage of nostalgia. I stared into the distance, into the dark and up at the disturbing abundance of stars. The night sky swung back and forth like a bell in an endless abyss of black. The blurry shapes on the inside, laughing, dancing, flipping through photos, showed no sign of missing my presence or my single lifestyle. To them, I was a high-functioning failure, absent of photos, nothing to parade.

I wiped my mouth with the shredded napkin and leaned against the deck railing with both hands, my head bowed forward and, as drunks do, gave myself permission to wallow in self-pity. A star shot across the blackness, searching for a place to fall. I am confused as to how stars can fill you with inspiration one moment and insignificance the next. "Lost, and by the wind grieved, ghost come back again." Shitfaced, I was still able to quote Thomas Wolfe. Mr. Igo's influence was alive and well.

My index finger stirred what was left of my drink and I found more questions to ask myself. How can the past be passed and still be as vivid as ever? Does the past even exist? If it is only what we remember, and memory is only a fraction of what the past was, what is real now and what was real then? Questions only a drunk would ask. I was worn out. It was time to go. What was that line? About the past? Hemmingway? Faulkner? "The past is never dead. It's not even past."

I felt as if I had stumbled into the beam of a slide projector, looking half exposed, poorly colored and quite ridiculous. My thoughts ricocheted from high school to the reunion and back with the same confusing questions. A missed signal? An explanation I failed to understand? "A stone. A leaf. An unfound door." Nothing ever clarified. Regret swept over me for all that is lost in youth. The moments of intimacy so tender, so naïve, squandered for lack of experience and obliviousness of mortality. Emotions that can never be recaptured. There is only ever one first time.

I walked back through the slider and for the first time noticed a couple at the far end of the deck and assumed they had witnessed my projectile into the azaleas. How could they not? Did I care? No.

I had to get out. I shouldered my way through the crowd toward the front door, through the noise of overlapping conversations now sounding like the desperate braying of everyone talking over everyone else. There would be no goodbyes. I hate endings. Always difficult for me. I cut farewells short. This time, I cut them out completely.

Betty, the girlfriend I'd avoided until now, ran into me face-to-face in the foyer. We were equally startled. She couldn't help but see the state I was in and grabbed both of my forearms as if to steady me. We stared hard at each other, as if we'd been in an extended conversation, the distress deepening the lines around my eyes, saying more than I could or was willing to.

"Richie, what on earth is wrong?"

"It's about the past," I said angrily, like an accusation, as if all of it, whatever *it* was, was her fault.

"What is?"

"Everything," I snapped. "Read the fine print."

"What fine print?" she replied, quizzically and a little insulted but tolerant, remembering the good times we'd had.

At least until I said, "The fine print! The fine print! The fine print where the truth is! Never what you expected!"

"Okay. Okay. Sorry I asked," and she turned and walked away. *She's grown hard,* I thought. *But she sure looks damn good in that dress! And the way she gripped my arms! Like she was expecting a kiss!*

I was caught between the large mirrors mounted on each side of the foyer. I glanced sideways. How incredibly inappropriate I was. A fool making no sense. I looked up at the clock duplicating and triplicating to infinity. The hands had stopped at three o'clock—the exact time I had cut the motor in front of Ken's house.

I left, taking the steps slowly, as if each one was more difficult from the last, *saudade* steering me and my mumbling to the car. "It is not enough that yearly, down this hill, April comes like an idiot, babbling and strewing flowers." Poetry and self-pity came easily, even, or rather, especially, in a maudlin state.

I climbed into the car, banging my head on the doorframe and falling into the seat like drunks do, as a blackout started to close in from all sides. The "spinners" stirred the bile in my stomach like silt in a pond. Everything started to revolve, slowly and then faster into the retching of an unprofitable but violent vomit. I threw the door open and leaned down toward the ground. Nothing in my stomach but twisted muscles and the convulsions of a dry heave. Thin strips of bile hung from my mouth. I laid my head back against the headrest, took a long, deep breath, and had some feeling of release, even a sense that something had been completed. As they had so many other times, those words came back: "Sometimes you just have to hold back." I'd never be rid of them. But now, the sting was different, not because I didn't understand what he had meant but because I understood it all too well.

———

Because I didn't see Jack age, to me he's still a teenager. He died in 2015 at the age of seventy-four, news that came to me as an afterthought from a former female classmate when we ran into each other at the gym. "And oh, by the way," she said following some mindless chitchat, "Jack died. Jack Swift. It was strange. A month later, so did Judy. Ironic, isn't it? Since they went steady in high school? Remember?"

I responded with a pensive, "Yes. I do remember." I stared off. To where I didn't know. As if she weren't there.

I bookmarked his obituary from the *Appeal-Democrat* in "My Favorites," the computer option where I add other important obituaries as I find them. I reread it from time to time, staring at a photograph I can't decode, projecting a fantasy pulling up remnants of the euphoria and slivers of the past. It reads longer than most. To me, the account is brief. His life looked full. There is much more I'd like to know. The chronology enumerated his virtues, as memorials do of the dead, when lives are reduced to milestones—college education, the career, wives, children, grandchildren, interests, etc., none of which sound like the boy I knew, the one I carried in my heart. But how little I knew him. And how poorly. He was in my life and then, like Bobby, he was gone, never knowing the better part of me, nor I him. I wish I could have said goodbye.

Jack was that rare person, one of a handful of others who, without knowing it, helped direct me toward my own identity. Life handed him to me, and others like him, just by living. He was like a foreign body, a graft, a patch that sent all the right impulses. Or the steel pin that keeps a broken bone together and as that and other bones healed, the path they put me on was more and more clear. And, as Robert Frost informed in "The Road Less Traveled": "I, I took the one less traveled by, and that has made all the difference." My road indeed.

CHAPTER 10

THE SEMEN TREE

NO MATTER HOW SMALL, no matter how insignificant or remote, any stimulus may, before you have time to think, take you back to another place and another time. It doesn't take much. A reflection in a store window. A chance feature on a stranger's face. A singular note of a bird in a tree. Or the tree itself. Or its falling blossoms.

They are complicated things, the memories that continue to accumulate. They are friends and, in a way, lovers, too, never quite as simple as you think, flashing unannounced onto the edge of your consciousness from some dark recess of the brain. *Lovers*, I call them, since, as with the most intimate relationships, they can be a great comfort or a troubling conflict, defying logic and from that hidden place take a circuitous route, dominating waking hours, taking you here rather than there—not at all where you imagined—on a course that follows not a straight line but one that defines its own journey and, like the human heart, is full of shadowy variations.

Those that come to me run the widest gamut—things as ordinary as a recent conversation or to the extreme of the mystical, as if I'd rubbed a magic lantern, the trail of smoke releasing a genie—all-knowing, all-seeing, and able to grant complex wishes. And no, reminiscence is not held together as simply as if it were one of the flowers in a vase where all the contents—the wilting flowers of experience—are bunched together, available to be plucked on demand. They could be memories from which I thought I had escaped, if escape is the right word, given how eagerly I have sought them out from time to time and how readily they are available. All configurations are possible, both real and imagined, from what is seen, heard, touched, or, in the particular instance I am about to describe, smelled. The nose remembers too.

It happened one day as I pulled into the parking lot of the Bel Air Market, a paved sea of blacktop. It was 2003, and I had returned to Yuba City, familiar to me the way hometowns are, with the memories of childhood appearing randomly here and there. The town had become foreign to the way my life had changed since I left. It was different and yet oddly the same, and it occurred to me that memories of home as a place had been replaced with home as simply an irrevocable condition. Sometimes at night, I tried to reach out and grab hold of what I had felt growing up there, but my thoughts were tangled. And sometimes, I'd drive down Brown Avenue past our old house and the Reeveses' and then out past the old Swift place, no longer standing, expecting to feel a certain way but instead just felt a slight and sudden sadness, not sure exactly what I expected. If it was a better understanding of the past, I was disappointed.

I had come back for a purpose and not with the reluctance I imagined I would have, given the eventuality of what brought me. I had returned to be available to my aging parents and to care for them, the circularity of life having reached that point when the hierarchy of a family reverses. The parent becomes the child; the child the parent. They needed my care as surely as I had once needed theirs.

Hard parts and hard decisions would come soon enough, but in the beginning my help was made of simple things—driving Dad to the ranch, watching his eyes scan the green fields of rice rolling in the wind with the admiration of a sea captain who marvels at the liquidity of the ocean. The sight of this connected him to his history, his life's work behind him now, but brought back as his eyes scanned the fields and his thoughts relived all he had accomplished and some he hadn't; my mother to her hair appointments or to visit a relative, the family social interaction always a joy; both parents to doctors' appointments, which were slowly but steadily becoming more frequent and more troubling. Mundane things like this don't seem to carry much significance as I list them now, but in their totality, they lent a sense of security and peace of mind for them and for me. They were not heroic gestures. It was simply payback time, which meant coming back to the hometown that had never been, nor ever would be, a good fit.

It was late spring, and the sprawling limbs of the Bradford pear tree shaded the parking lot. The blossoms, heavy in white clusters, were nearly bloomed out and had begun to fall, covering the parked cars and asphalt like a blanket of light snow in a pointillist painting. With the windows of the car rolled down, the aroma off the trees filled my nose with a smell unlike other spring flowers, familiar but strange. That in turn set off a flurry of images that became not just one but a litany of remembered experience, relating to each other loosely in that they occurred in tandem, like a length of uncultured pearls on a string that are graduated in size and shape and value.

The Latin name, *Pyrus calleryana*, offers no clue as to the peculiar characteristic, this unexpected smell. The tree itself is a contradiction, developed by man as a freak of nature almost. Like the flowering quince and the fruitless mulberry, it bears no fruit, developed to be decorative and barren. But when cross-pollinated with other cultivars of callery pears, it self-modifies and produces thorny thickets and thorny fruit, the seeds of which are eaten and disseminated by birds. Then it turns invasive, wild, and unruly, like the memories that appear unwanted, pests in your own psychological thicket.

In contrast to the usual green and fertile smells of spring, the sweet ones that fill your head with thoughts of romance and the promise of new beginnings, this one is neither pleasant nor unpleasant, but tucked somewhere in between familiar, foreign, sharp, musty, slightly acrid, and a bit salty with a trace element of sweet. In a word, it smells like cum. The provocative nickname "the semen tree" is no surprise if you've ever . . . never mind.

Once this notion registered, the thoughts that followed were inconsistent in a way but, in a way, not. I was in high school, a freshman, and in gym class. And then. And then. And when memory chooses, it is bound neither to smooth transitions nor logic. One thought may relate to another or not at all. The mechanism of the mind can switch from blossoms to semen to gym class to other places and other times. So, in the parking lot, I embarked on a mystery tour, in which many stops occurred one after another in rapid and illogical succession.

The blossoms, withering and warm and redolent of cum, moved effortlessly to thoughts of the locker room after gym class, a place of firm-featured boys and a conglomerate, pulsing male presence where masculinity is worn as unequivocally as skin and provocative behavior, suggestive and prurient came naturally with no thought or apology, no fear of recrimination or blowback. The throbbing physicality was overwhelming. Sweaty jockstraps, yellow gym shorts, and Honkers T-shirts thrown carelessly on the cement floor alongside tennis shoes, underwear-crisp, JCPenney's tighty-whities, checkered boxers, or hash-marked off brands; to naked bodies, flaccidly arrogant dicks anxious to be admired; other nakedness, less bold, anxious and unsure, covering itself with a hand or a towel to the occasional jibe—"Hey, girlie boy, whatcha got hidin' under that towel? Not much, huh?"—a taunt or a challenge. The trek to the white-tiled, heartless communal shower where the confident and the self-conscious have to mix, equal only in the fact that they're naked and exposed and where a sideways glance, if held too long, could be interpreted as desire, that dangerous betrayer of secrets, and lead to rumors and the death of social reputations.

For me to find a comfortable slot in all this was nearly beyond my capability given the circumstance. I read sexual overtones, real or imagined, in body language in every corner, arousing me against my better judgment but nearly out of my control. Casting furtive glances at jockstrapped crotches dwelling on what was cupped within was an indulgence I couldn't afford.

But fitting in was the key to popularity, a vitally important status. (Wasn't being unpopular, in some minor way, a demonstration of the world telling you that you are dispensable? That the world can get along just fine without you?) Navigating the locker room was part of fitting in, even though the physicality and the proximity put me at odds with myself, unspeakable inclinations coiled inside like a spring. The guillotine of social consequence being what it was, and the fear of it so dizzying, there was only one solution, one way around it. Cloak desire. Deny self.

Jack was in this class and had the same aversion to the communal shower as I had. More paranoic because of the birthmark, the shocking mar on his otherwise fine body. We raced to the locker room from different places on the field—him from a team sport, me from whatever out-of-the-way place I came from, often reaching the building the same time, in and out of the showers before the rest of the class got there with a quick wet-down and cursory drying-off, facing in opposite directions. We'd be dressed and leaving as the class was arriving. If our eyes met, as they sometimes did, there was more than self-consciousness there—something beyond the awkwardness of the circumstance. You know about that. This was before the rite of spring.

My behavior in the claustrophobia of the steamy locker room was because of what I'd been taught, although "taught" is not exactly the right word when it came to the body and sex. Nothing on this subject was articulated. It was absorbed by osmosis—mostly from the Nazarenes, although both sides of the family shared dirty hands on this. Since the naked body smacked of sin, it was never spoken about. If seen, it was by accident. It was never, ever flaunted—swimming suits excepted, which made little sense. Your body was yours in the bathroom. You did with it what you wanted and never discussed it. I saw the body as a beautiful thing. For my family, it was a subject they avoided, since temptation lurked there. All because Adam and Eve had eaten the apple.

The unavoidable sense of maleness in the room had an accumulated presence of boys feeling the intoxicating power of manhood, inexplicably satisfying and sending off a deep flutter in me. It's the intoxication sweat gives to skin. Temptation was close. The fruit from the tree was low-hanging. Cocks, balls, asses, washboard abs—they were everywhere. Flexing muscles, body parts soaped up, rinsed off, dripping, toweled, and damp were land mines within arm's reach.

A bare butt. The crack of a wet towel. An open invitation to ogle and evaluate. "Watch it, asshole." Or a litany of smart remarks and put-downs. "Hey, lard ass, get a move on." Or "Bite me." "In your dreams." "Hey, outta the way, pencil penis!"

You wonder about me: How did this make me feel? The annoying, unyieldingly repetitive question asked on the 24-7 news programs of today's television. "How did it make you feel?" "How did it make you feel?" Fuck! I didn't know how I felt. I was aroused. I was thrilled. I was terrified of my thoughts, ones that flirted with danger and the thrill of proximity. The conjunction of fear and arousal at odds with each other. I was afraid. I was paranoid.

That is not to say there weren't snapshot moments that could have been catastrophic. I remember one specifically. A boy, popular and athletic, whose nickname was "The Rope" because of his unusual endowment, stood in the locker room nearby where I was sitting, waiting for his area to thin out. His towel was holding together, sitting low on his pelvis bones, the two twisted ends trying to come undone. He'd dried off from showering and he was leaning against the wall near his locker with his arms folded across his chest and caught me staring at the downward curving length pushing out from the flat surface of his towel. During the brief interval when our eyes were locked, the towel came loose and fell to the ground. I should have looked away and let what I saw appear to be a moment of disinterested curiosity and nothing more, but I didn't. I looked from his crotch to his face, the square, hard stubbornness of his jaw, and into the softness of his blue eyes. He glanced down at himself and then back at me and smiled. That was all. He could have as easily said, in a way that would have drawn a lot of attention, "What the fuck are *you* staring at?" Instead, he just picked up the towel, wrapped it back around his waist, and went about his business.

The hetero "subtext," the macho male in this scenario, seems clearer to me now. The "bonding" and "sharing" between males on the field during team sports have implications now I didn't see then. The intense clench of bodies in the football huddle, tacitly alluring, justified by the rules of the game, the circle of bunched, moist jockstraps cupping acrid genitals and flexing muscles that emitting the smell of rotting weeds in a small, sunny mud puddle. Weren't there sexual implications somewhere in the patting-each-others-asses scenario? Weren't urges stimulated by the physicality inherent in sports? Rushing, grabbing, pushing, tackling, body-to-body contact, probable, rough, aggressive, and brutal? The thin, sadomasochistic thread in the very nature of sports. A delayed predilection satisfied at a later time in some other way? Masturbation? Screwing a girlfriend? Or would the shower be the buffer? The cooling off? The acceptable and temporary denouement.

So what was my place in the great panorama of gym class? That question was answered soon after my first day as a high school freshman, class of 1954.

———

My arrival was anticipated in much the same way Bobby's had been. The athletic department knew all about me. By the time I walked up the steps to Yuba City High, I was a local celebrity, my notoriety as a national roller-skating champion firmly established. Every summer since the fifth grade, I had competed in annual state, regional, and national competitions, earning titles in all three divisions several years running.

Inverted camel spin, 1957.

After school, I practiced or took lessons or both. I skated night sessions several days during the week. A lot of weekend time was spent there. And, oddly or not, I found a place in a collection of eccentric personalities, from which I had developed attitudes and behaviors the same way I absorbed family culture and school mores. Compared to my high school friends, the ones I had at the skating rink were a marked departure in many ways. They added a different perspective to life in general. The odd and eccentric group seemed normal and the characters as colorful as the high school faculty. And I was the youngest, at an age where a couple of years difference can seem the difference between the naïve and the sophisticated. The skating rink crowd gave me a one-up on sophistication that high school didn't, and a look at some of the individuals will show why.

Ruby, the owner's wife, breastfed her baby in the office that had windows of glass on three sides. She sat in full public view, with no compunction about showing her pendulous tit to everyone buying a ticket.

There was a cross-dressing accordion player who gave music lessons by day and by night dressed as a woman and picked up soldiers at the bar of the Olympic Hotel, and who also was cast in drag, usually a Carmen Miranda–type character, in our annual skating production.

There was an older, questionable man who worked for a while as a soda jerk in the coffee shop. He thought it clever to show a phony photo of a baby smoking a cigarette and laughed until he cried when he pulled the picture out of his wallet and showed the bottom half, which presented an erect penis half the length of the baby's entire body.

There was a family that won baby ducks at the carnival and kept them in the bathtub of their two-bedroom duplex until they, the ducks, were fully grown.

There was a skating associate of mine, beautiful and always smartly dressed with more cashmere sweaters that I had, also a national champion, who accepted her titles as if they made her real royalty. I will never forget the condescending compliment she gave me from her throne once, looking down on me as a noble would a peasant. She said, "You know, you are really very sweet . . . in your own little way," emphasis on *little*. This lady was and still is a legend in her own mind, a local Norma Desmond, her close-up, Mr. DeMille, having come and was long gone. There were more eccentric types at the rink, all of whom I thought of as normal. Association with them made me more sophisticated and worldly—in my mind, anyway.

My collection of ribbons and trophies *was* impressive. The sports section of the local paper, the *Appeal Democrat*, had featured me on its front page. I had been interviewed on KUBA, the local radio station, when I was eleven or twelve, before my voice changed. (In the playback, much to my mortification, I sounded like a young girl, the memory of which makes me cringe as I write this.) Sometimes I was stopped for an autograph. I was talented. I knew it. I was riding high. I had everything I wanted but not everything I needed. Time revealed this, as time does all things.

I didn't wear fame well. Didn't handle success with grace. I was conceited, arrogant, entitled, sarcastic, and condescending—a veneer of my own construct and one that didn't serve me as well as I thought. I was too shallow to see through the transparency of my behavior and too young to become bored with my own self-centeredness, an ability

I would acquire later in life, even though at this point in life, it is still nearly impossible to divert my mind completely away from my moods.

Unattractive behavior aside, I was relatively popular. Why, a mystery to me now. A good sense of humor? Nice clothes? More V-necked sweaters than anyone in school? Because I had a car at my disposal when nobody else did? No doubt the car was a factor, although it pains me to think that.

The bold-faced truth was I didn't like the way I looked—not my face or my body. I did what insecure people, adults as well as children, do—present as the exact opposite. I know, I know. A national skating champion would be in pretty good physical shape. I was. And as I study my high school picture from the distance of time, I was a pretty good-looking kid. But we rarely see ourselves as others do, our self-perceptions sometimes at a remove from everyone else. I compared myself to what was *out there* in Hollywood and the movies, mostly. There was a constant barrage of unreal, impossible imagery. And also confusion: fantasy versus reality—the perfect chasm to remain confused in. Quoting Blanche DuBois, "I don't want reality. I want magic." I suppose that was me. And there was, as always, the prevailing memory of Bobby, naked.

So, what does this have to do with gym class? My ego left me ill-prepared for the ability I not only sorely lacked at team sports but the fact that I failed miserably at every one of them. It was a very bitter pill to swallow, and it lodged firmly in my throat like a big piece of meat. My psyche had been doused with big bucket of ice water. I choke on the thought of it now.

A double salchow. A split-flip. A flying camel. Piece of cake. These I could do on skates. No problem. But hitting baseballs or shagging flies or fielding ground balls or dribbling, blocking, or tackling? No way. This was not within my capability. Coordination on skates meant zilch as a team player and, as they say in French, *Les jeux sont faits*—The die is cast.

The die for me was cast. One dismal performance followed another, and I was either the last one chosen when teams were made up or second to last to Willy Williamson, a kid who wore his gym shorts so high a testicle might hang out the side and who would constantly push on a door marked "Pull." (Years later, I found out that he had found his way to the altar, even though he had never shown much interest in girls other that the occasional mutter, "Nice boobs," to himself when he skittered by a busty girl in the hall.) It didn't seem possible, but he was a worse athlete than I was. The fact of sitting next to him on the bench, knowing I was the last or next to last to be chosen, was almost more than I could bear.

But I could run fast. My legs were strong from skating. It didn't help my standing as a team player, but I could outrun anyone who might get on my case for being a fuckup.

Gym wasn't all bad. There were some good times. I just can't remember them. They are not in my immediate file of high school experience. And, as I have established, being Portuguese and a Pisces, as in my sense of humor, I lean toward the darker side of life, or the dreamy and romantic, not the banal jock "hum-babe" stuff.

Attendance in class had an effect on grades, including phys ed. I was in the small category of straight-A students, fully intending to stay there: (1) because of my overachiever syndrome, the need to please and not disappoint, and (2) pragmatically, for admission to a good college, an important goal I never lost sight of. Only so many passes to the nurse's office would fly before grades would suffer. So, what I did, what I had to do, was find a way to get through the hour as painlessly as I could, which meant becoming, if not invisible, then inconspicuous. There were plausible ways to do this: avoiding eye contact with the coaches; finding a reason, any reason, to hold back from assembling groups by stopping to fix a shoelace; replacing faulty equipment; run to the john when I didn't have to. Anything to fade into the background—not all that difficult, as it turned out, and, curiously, it taught me an important fact of life: it doesn't take much to go unnoticed when you are neither wanted nor needed. I was both, giving rise to a neurosis I struggled with in analysis for years—the need to be wanted as proof of my existence.

Two classmates became co-conspirators in the how-to-get-out-of-gym effort. Together, we found ways to avoid class whenever and wherever we could. Harold Crowhurst and Johnny-I-can't-remember-his-last-name. Like me, they were as indifferent to athletics as I was averse to it, with no qualms about truancy. Goldbricking was more or less a badge of honor.

During the frenzy of the teams scattering to different areas of the playing fields, one by one we'd sneak under the bleachers of the football stadium and spend the hour in hiding there, lying in a circle with our heads propped up on one hand picking tufts of grass or our noses, or pulling at our crotches to readjust what was held hostage in our jockstraps. Conversation, peppered with incessant wisecracking, was whatever nonsense went through the heads. We bragged about things we were going to do with no intention of ever doing them. If someone had managed to sneak a few cigarettes, we'd smoke. Or just lie around like dulled cows grazing. And as happens with teenage boys, we'd get erections for no apparent reason, if not simultane-ously, then one prompted by the other, all clearly outlined against our yellow gym shorts. *Harold has a really great dick,* I thought to myself. *I wish I had his dick.* I could get a boner in the blink of an eye. Just a thought would do it, like reflecting on what I'd seen in the locker room, Eddie Christensen's handsome face and luxurious head of blond hair combed in a ducktail, Dickie Brumfield's bubble butt. Anything could do it. In an of itself, hard-ons weren't the problem. It's what you did, or didn't do, with them. If, for instance, we jacked ourselves off, it might be okay. But if, in turns, we jacked each other off, would we have crossed that intangible boundary of propriety? Just how far could we go? It was hard (no pun) to know. This was an area of very thin ice, precariously close to that social no-man's-land where the guillotine of unacceptable behavior falls and you are forever separated from the social strata you so hungrily crave. And even if what happened had no actual sex in it, it was clearly suffused with eros and the danger of what could have happened next.

"We'd better get back," I'd say, thinking I had more to lose than they did should things take a turn for the worse, or better, depending on how you look at it. We left our grassy hiding place, our erections dying as erections do, and returned to the fringes of class with no trace of what had been or what might have been. To this day, I wonder what thoughts Harold and Johnny had. Would they have liked to stay a bit longer out of sight, out of mind, and, literally, in touch? Did they have the same urge that I did? Would they have turned themselves over to inclination and desire, as I might have? Were they afraid of thoughts like that? Did they know secrecy and desire are often one?

Our threesome did not extend past the hour of PE. Our social circles didn't overlap. So the what-ifs never went beyond the bleachers. With two notable exceptions. Harold and I had a couple of—what shall I call them—assignations? One in class and one out. But the word suggests they were planned when they weren't. "Spontaneous interludes" might be more accurate.

One during a film when gym class had been rained out. I don't remember the subject—something boring, I'm sure, on self-improvement or national parks or *What the Army Can Do for You*. However, I got some self-improvement without the army having to do a thing for me when Harold jerked me off under the table at the far end of the darkened, curtained room.

And the second on another rainy day when I got another hand job from him in the back row of the State Theater during a Saturday matinee of *Pete Kelly's Blues,* a movie that starred Jack Webb. (For those who don't know or are too young to remember, Webb was the star of the successful television series *Dragnet*, with its familiar tagline, "Just the facts, ma'am. We just want the facts.")

———

My cell phone rang about eight thirty on an evening after I'd given my mother her pallid dinner of a small, skinless chicken breast, a couple of tablespoons of frozen peas, and instant mashed potatoes without butter. It was one of the few tasteless dishes she would consider and only then a few bites from each food group. The voice was deep and slightly slurred but one I recognized although it had been twenty-five years since we had spoken.

"Hello," I said, annoyed that anyone would call at that hour. Age made me irritable when my evening television schedule was interrupted.

"Richie? It's Betty," the voice said.

"My Betty?" I answered, knowing full well who this Betty was.

"Yes," she said, a little surprised I recognized her and then, not. From there, our conversation soared with questions and recollections as if we'd just seen each other the day before. Some connections in life are that way.

The reason she called was about an upcoming class reunion. Another one. This time our fiftieth.

"I'll go if you will," I suggested. And she did. We spent the entire evening together in a wonderful, warm reminiscence of high school and the part we had played in each other's life—then and the unresolved feelings that had clung to us after that, such a different experience from the calamitous Peach Tree encounter twenty-five years before.

This time, the reunion was decidedly quieter, more sedate, and with much less drinking than the last one I'd been to. We all were in or near the grandparent stage of life, with its corresponding changes in physical appearance. Men were taking pills for swollen prostate, including myself, and women were well past menopause, not to mention other age-related conditions invisible to the naked eye. We moved around at the pace nature had given us by then.

The reunion had been moved from the swanky-ish Peach Tree Country Club to the Bonanza Inn, a small, off-the-beaten-path motel with a banquet room that was adequate for our current number, which had dwindled. This time, the milestone was measured largely by two different but related sureties: those who were still alive, and those who weren't.

The Grim Reaper had come and gone many times, leaving considerably fewer participants in this celebration, if celebration it could be called. It was as much about who wasn't there as who was. Respects were paid to those who'd passed as we all held hands and all their names were read. It was a long list. The soup had gotten cold. And the entrees hadn't changed. Still your choice, prepaid, of gray roast beef or chicken cordon bleu, vegetarian if requested ahead of time as a special order.

Earlier, I'd run into Harold Crowhurst as I approached the building. He'd stepped out to have a smoke. It was the first time I'd seen him since we'd graduated. While I can't remember the exact words of our exchange, the essence of it was something like this:

Me: Hey . . . er . . .*(If it's Harold, he's gained a lot of weight,* I thought.) . . . Harold?

Harold (pulling the smoke from a lit cigarette deep into his lungs, holding it as if he were holding his breath before exhaling. His toothy grin identifies him. Without a doubt. It's Harold. A grin doesn't gain weight.): Yeah.

Me: Been a long time.

Harold: Yeh.

Harold has always been a man of few words.

A pause was charged with disinterest, telling me our conversation was going to be filled with more indifference than questions.

Me: So, how've you been?

Harold (after some consideration): Good. You?

Me: Can't complain. Nobody'd listen anyway. Right?

Harold (another pause, as if he had to think about it): Right.

Then I ask the obvious question. The easy one.

Me: You married? (*Of course he's married. What a dumb question!*)

Harold: Yeah. Five sons.

Me: Wow. Busy guy.

Harold (grins): Yeah. (His next question. The obvious one.) You?

Me (I pause and look him in the eye, toying with an idea. Should I tell him why?): Nah. Never got around to it.

And I'm thinking now would be a good time to leave. Before he got to the "How come?" part; also thinking that he's suspecting the *how come*, although in high school, his thinking never seemed to go that deep. So maybe not. Knowing I'd never see him again, the little guy on my shoulder with the pitchfork was goading me in his devilish way to nudge Harold in the ribs and whisper from the corner of my mouth, looking off to the side as though it was our little secret, "Remember that day in *Pete Kelly's Blues*? You and me?" I didn't. We shifted our respective weight from one foot to another, started looking down and around—anywhere to avoid further eye contact. The conversation had stalled by mutual consent.

Me: Guess I'll see you . . . inside.

He grinned again. Harold was one of those guys who smiled when there was nothing to smile about. Like Mr. Reeves, but innocently. As I turned and walked toward the building, I marveled that he had not lost that consummate voice, the one that would have given him a fine career on FM radio. I saw him in the reflection of the glass doors, taking a fresh drag on his cigarette. I wondered, as I entered the building, whether any of his five sons ever played around under the bleachers or anyplace else. A year later, in 2009, I read in the paper that Harold had died of a heart attack.

It's hard to think that all this came from withering spring blossoms. But it did. The last thought I had before I left the car to do the shopping was to visualize the tree that had been near the Bonanza when Harold and I had our talk—a Bradford pear—like those surrounding me then. Not in bloom and not the least bit aromatic, the season well over, and the leaves turning, about to fall.

Funny, what you remember. And what you forget. For a time too brief to measure, I had been temporarily drawn away from the reason I'd returned home and had had a moment to dwell on some of the reasons why I left in the first place.

CHAPTER 11

ONE LAST QUESTION,
AND OTHER THINGS

DAYS AND DAYS AND DAYS PASS, some without a sound, until there are no days left. That's how it happens as days swallow themselves one after another in rapid succession. In the business of life, you have accumulated the memories, those you still are able to retain, and in the end, that's all there is—a slim storehouse of what you can still recall. You have crossed the minefield of middle age, the transition into old age coming so quickly after taking so long. Before you realize it, you come to the end of your life and the end of your story. You've lived too long and too much. There is nothing left to say. You have been stricken with the final disease for which there is no cure: old age, during which for X number of days, weeks, months, years, you transcend the rest of the world and become a race apart from the race you were once a part of.

Perhaps you've laid some chapters down, as I have done, or simply kept them in your head, your trove of memory, that place where your nows have given way to your thens. You reflect on the lifetime mural you painted, seeing how some things were more important than you realized and some far less than you wanted, many not what you'd hoped. There are no new people to meet, and you prefer instead the memory of your dead in a great cemetery where the names on the tombstones are becoming less and less readable. You have become one of what Ezra Pound called "old men with beautiful manners."

And now there is the lingering question: Have I remembered things as they were, or as I wanted them to be, or how I hope they had been? Either way, there is finally an ending, some experiences too far in the past to know the real truth of what they were.

And there you are. Old, having crossed that murky divide between old age and dark old age when, as King Lear says, we "crawl toward death." Sleep becomes the kindest friend, the most tender lover. Marooned in a hospital bed. Alone with people around you. Breaths away from being ultimately and finally alone in a coffin. Friends and relatives come. Then dwindle. Then don't come at all, agreeing it is better not to.

It was August 2010. Leaves had begun an early turn from green to yellow, orange, and bright red, dying but not quietly. In a few months, my mother would be in her ninety-fifth year. An old cautionary voice from the cage that still carped "I told you so" whispered what I already felt in my gut. It was not likely we would be celebrating her birthday. She was well beyond the point where new experiences would be made or new excitements felt; rather, old ones revisited, some with fondness, and others with regret, and often speaking of what was gone forever as if it were still in the room; the mere wish to do something now as good as the actual doing of it. She was at that point where living itself seemed to be an insufficient incentive to go on living.

Over the last two years, the twenty pounds she had lost during recovery from two pressure fractures in her vertebrae—the result of advanced osteoporosis—had been gained back, pound by stubborn pound, a victory hard won. But, abruptly, the weight began melting away almost before our eyes, day by day, for several weeks. The digital numbers on the bathroom scale raced ahead, bounced back and forth, slowing and stopping at seventy-seven, seventy-six, seventy-five pounds. She stepped off the scale and onto what was to be a final crossroad. Part of me was not prepared for the truth. Another part knew with resounding clarity she was in crisis.

Mom after Dad's funeral, 2004.

As I woke her up for her doctor's appointment, I thought to myself that even when she was sleeping, she was better than most women I knew. She was in the family room recliner, her chair of choice these days in a piece of furniture that now seemed to engulf her in three separate pieces rather than cradle her as a whole. Most days and many nights would find her staring at the television screen, the images a blur, jumps of reality, with the volume turned to 10—voices that were simply sounds she didn't really listen to. Or she would be sleeping with her mouth agape, a transitory escape from the deepening haze of dementia, a condition we joked about in earlier years when forgetfulness was something to laugh at. Some days were better than others, but those were fewer and fewer, having merely become fluctuations of a steady decline.

"Time to go, Mom," I said in a voice that could have been construed as shouting. She was hard of hearing.

"Huh? What?" she responded, disoriented from just waking up, and not fully realizing where she was.

"Your appointment. Remember? Dr. Inamura today."

Although it was summer and still hot, she was bundled in a sweater as we left the house. I helped her out the laundry room door to the car, carefully navigating the two concrete steps to the garage floor where, from her walker, she grunted and twisted herself into the passenger seat of the Mercury Marquis she could no longer drive. The night had been warm, and the stuffy air of the garage hovered around us like a suffocating blanket.

"Where we goin'?" she asked again.

"The doctor," I repeated. This back and forth happened all the time. I was used to it. Not really.

Simple activities that had always been taken for granted had become tedious and potentially dangerous. No matter how routine, nothing was routine anymore. Two constant companions, dementia and osteoporosis, saw to that, as they escorted her to the toilet or to the car, or when she walked down the hall or wandered out to the mailbox, forgetting where she was. They were permanent attachments now, closer to her than even her two sons or her grandson.

Compared to the rest of her generation, Mom had been one of the luckier ones in the family. She had navigated life gracefully, stoically, two qualities she still clung to, her quiet, unaggressive opinion offered only after considered hesitation. The waves of family deaths in the last ten-odd years had come and gone. Small tsunamis of loss every family endures, Mom enduring hers with silent stoicism and quiet resignation. Even the most important one, sudden and shocking, passed in relative silence, leaving things still to be said.

"Marie, I'm dying," my father murmured matter-of-factly, as he slumped over the steering wheel of that same Mercury Marquis we were sitting in at the moment. The two of them were in the parking lot of the Waffle Hut. A massive heart attack took him down, swiftly, silently, with her sitting next to him in the passenger seat. The tears she shed for this loss were quiet ones, and few, as far as I could tell. And a comment she made once to a friend comes back to me for no reason at all, as thoughts do. "Sometimes I feel like no one in the world loves me," she said in a plaintive, quiet voice. And I wondered if anyone at all, including myself, knew who my mother was, who she really was.

The loss of my father was loss of that moment between fathers and sons when the opportunity to say all that should have been said is gone. He could never know me as the person I'd been or the person I'd become. Unless the same is true for fathers as for mothers: mothers always know. At any rate, the opportunity was gone. The things we never said were now buried in our yesterdays.

Mom and Dad, circa 1955.

I almost took the phone off the hook and laid it on the nightstand and tried to ignore the persistent ringing when I finally muttered, "For fuck's sake," and fumbled for the receiver. "Yes?" I said.

"Herr Souza? *Bitte?* This is the desk. You have the collect call from California. You make to accept the charges, *bitte?*" the hotel operator asked in her heavy German accent.

"Yes," I replied, half asleep, half awake, adrenalin beginning to pump in that way a phone call in the middle of the night in a hotel room in a foreign country affects your heart rate. It was October 2004. The call was from a friend my mother had called who somehow had managed to find me. It was to pass on the news of my father's death.

After I hung up, I can't remember what came first—grief or, as much as I am ashamed to say, a sense of relief that I'd never have to search for the right words, because there would have been no right words to tell him, without apology, who I was and how I had lived my life, fearing I would be his, and my mother's, great disappointment, the confidence that they both could love me in spite of my sexual preference a void in my consciousness. I felt guilty but also guiltily free—a weighty emotion that would come again, to a lesser degree, with my mother's death. And I didn't cry.

I caught the next plane home. I didn't cry during the numbed decision-making: picking the coffin, ordering the flowers, arranging the caterer for the gathering after the funeral. I didn't view his body in the coffin. No matter what anyone says, given the waxen look the undertaker constructs, the dead never look like themselves, even laid out in their best. I didn't want the last impression I would have of my father to be a gray, artificial visage. It wasn't until the quiet days that followed that I accepted he was gone for good. And that the silence between us, the one pervasive in our family that we could never break, the one in which we hid emotions, was permanent. We'd had a lifetime of practice. I'd missed the chance to have conversations with either my mother or father on subjects we'd managed to avoid all our lives. Then I cried.

Dementia had established its unrelinquishable, irreversible grip on my mother. I would hear the same questions from her over and over again. "Whose house is this?" Or "What day is this? I forget." Or "Is this my house?" Happily, the other growing incapacity, macular degeneration, never prompted the question "Who are you?" She knew everyone to the end, as long as the face facing her was close enough. But suddenly she would be gone, dislocated, returned to whatever time she inhabited at that moment.

Sometimes she'd surprise us. "I'd really like to go to New York someday," coming from nowhere. "Mom, we went two years ago. Remember? You fell asleep during the first act of *The Lion King*." After a minute's reflection when I could see her thinking hard, "Oh yes. Of course," she replied. Maybe she had remembered. Maybe not. It didn't matter.

———————

"Where are those damn keys?" I said after I had gotten in the driver's seat. I thought, *Okay. I'm headed for the gaga room,* and went back into the house to find the keys exactly where I had left them, next to the landline phone on the kitchen counter. I could remember every word of "Why Do Fools Fall in Love," but I couldn't remember what I went to the store for. As I said, the gaga room. Pausing at the kitchen counter, stopping for no reason to glance at the phone in its cradle, I remembered the phone in our house on Brown Avenue and my fifth birthday and the picture taken of me on my birthday present, the Shetland pony, Poncho. The Brown Avenue house with the black party-line phone. "Number, please," the operator said. What comes to mind. And when. Always a surprise.

We drove across the old bridge to Dr. Inamura, her primary physician, a visit that turned out to be her final one and the last time she would leave her own house. She sat next to me passively, looking shrunken in her shrunken world, a small bundle of curved, porous bones. I had to smile as I glanced over at her though. She was a quintessential time warp with heavily spray-netted hair, each back-combed strand lacquered to within an inch of its life, the silvery white beehive a living relic from the 1960s—washed, rinsed, dyed, dried, backcombed, and sprayed into its original configuration every Thursday, ten o'clock, at Rosemary's Wig and Beauty Salon by Rosemary herself ("I'm a beautician, not a magician!"), one of many family nieces by marriage. Loyalty to family was also one of Mom's qualities. She would never think of ever using anyone but Rosemary.

Outside the car, wisps of air moved tentatively, easily, but I felt something ominous hanging on the fringe of the breeze, an intuition that came and went before I had time to give it form. The twinge it produced was interrupted by our familiar, predictable exchange.

"Sure is a nice day," she said while looking out the window. After a pause, "What day is it?"

"Tuesday, Mom." Another pause.

"What town are we in?" She'd lived here her entire life.

"Yuba City, Mom."

"Oh. I forgot." Pause. "Where're we going?"

"Dr. Inamura's, Mom." Her brows furrowed as she struggled to formulate another thought. Then moved on to the first accessible one.

"Wonder how Vera's doin'."

Conversation had gotten harder to handle. My impatience grew thin as my guilt grew stronger and as the same conversations were inevitably repeated over and over again. I wasn't proud of the way I felt. It was some kind of betrayal, some kind of mental abandonment that I could neither define nor help feeling. I took a deep breath. Flatly, "Mom, Annie (the pronunciation the family used for "Auntie") Vera died last year. Remember?" I took another deep breath and thanked the gods for yoga.

"Oh . . . I forgot." She stared out the window, and I could see she went to a familiar, comfortable place. "Sure is a nice day. I really like the trees."

The small rural hospital, where I'd had my tonsils out and in which the doctor's office was located, had grown since the 1940s into a medical conglomerate, the corporate machine having slowly, methodically devoured three adjacent city blocks of small businesses and homes and now was in yet another phase of expansion. The hospital had grown aloof from the neighborhood it dominated and stood like an enormous Erector set with huge steel beams and girders rising with quiet stealth beside existing buildings and dwarfing them.

Doctor Inamura's office was tucked in one wing along with a score of other doctors' offices—tiny cogs in the large wheel of what was simply called *Rideout* by the locals. ("Oh, of course. They took her straight to Rideout.") The rural hospital was now officially the Rideout Regional Medical Center.

Illness needed more and more room in which to groan and convalesce. As the profit margin grew, the needs were met with cement, steel, plaster, pastel paint, innocuous prints, and elevator music as each patient waited their turn in the waiting rooms, disrobing for examination, being diagnosed with this or that, given good news, bad news, or no news ("Let's see you in two weeks"), medications prescribed as indicated. In another part of the hospital complex, bodies were being shaved in any number of places—chest, crotch, thighs, heads—in preparation for surgeries. And in another, supine bodies on dollies were being wheeled into recovery rooms, or for the end-of-the-liners, being pronounced DOA after paramedics screeched up to emergency entrances.

I helped my mother from the car to her walker, and we shuffled forward with my hand guiding her elbow, our heads bent down against a spontaneous gust of wind from the north, or from no origin at all, charged with electricity, the vexing kind that dries out lawns and plants in half a day. An infant twister swirled in circles, angrily worrying our faces with dust and leaves, discarded gum wrappers and other detritus, and forcing tree limbs to bend with disturbing messages scratched by their dry leaves against the asphalt.

Mom was weak from weight loss and atrophy. Her legs gave out before we reached the automatic door that opened and then closed perfunctorily after the programmed interval, oblivious to our circumstance, not caring whether or not we had crossed its threshold. I picked her up in my arms, leaving the walker stranded, and stepped toward the door, which opened again with no judgment, no opinion. I carried her down the long hall off the foyer where multiple office doors stood face-to-face, closed to each other. Different doctors. Different needs. In my arms, she was weightless as a straw stick figure. Held close but gingerly to my chest, she felt as brittle as a baby bird just dry from its shell.

In my imagination, a phantom gust of wind snatched the tissue paper body from my arms, spinning it into the air, twirling it around like a discarded Kleenex, and then vanished, *whoosh,* as quickly as it had come, crashing her to the ground and disintegrating before my eyes into a small pile of light gray powder.

"DNR. DO NOT RESUSCITATE." The note Scotch-taped to the refrigerator door flashed on my inner eye, my veins pulsing hard like arteries engorged with blood. "I think you should have this—that is, if you agree, of course." The doctor had scribbled the directive in spastic illegibility on his prescription pad during our previous visit. "Make copies and put them in several places throughout the house. Anywhere a 911 team might see them. Even moderate CPR would crush the sternum and ribs. There would be nothing we could do. In the worst-case scenario, if she didn't die then, we couldn't do much for her from then on. It would be out of our hands. If she lived, life would be hell for her—and worse than hell for the family—on morphine twenty-four seven. Not dead, but for all intents and purposes, not really alive—until she died—feeding tube, IVs, the whole thing. The suffering would be unimaginable . . ." His remembered words trailed off as I came back to present time with my mother still curled in my arms.

I started down the hall. One of the doctor's office staff stepped out just as we got to the door. Startled, she said, "Oh. Oh! Here. Let me get a wheelchair for you."

"Just the door," I said.

We were lucky. There was no need to wait in the waiting room. The doctor appeared as though he were expecting us even before I could put my mother into a chair. Bad news travels fast. He motioned to the nearest examination room.

Dr. Inamura was a medium-sized man of medium build with thick black hair peppered with gray, combed straight back from his forehead. His manner had the quiet but firm authority of the medical profession, and his Japanese heritage gave his voice an edge of Asian gentility.

"We're not doing so well today, I see. What seems to be the problem?" he said closing the door behind him. Sardonically, I think, *You've been Mom's physician for forty years, for Christ's sake, and you don't have some idea what the problem is?* But I said nothing, deferring, as I did, to the authority of doctors, lawyers, and the police—residual baggage from my upbringing.

There was nothing particularly different in the doctor's manner this time, but my nerves were frayed and what he was saying, or rather the way he was saying it, was as irritating as my mother's repeated questions. I bit my tongue. I filled him in as best I could on what he had, I was sure, already surmised. He listened with professional dispassion, nodding with robotic concern.

"Okay. Let's have a look," he said, handing my mother the thin blue gown, the ones with the large hospital arm holes and that tie in three places at the back. "I'll be back in a minute and we'll see what we can do." He stepped out of the room as he said this. *We* did not mean my mother and him and me. *We* smacked, I thought, of the *royal we*. This also annoyed me. I kept it to myself too.

"Can't seem to get these buttons," she complained, fumbling at the front of her flannel blouse. I undid them for her, noticing, as I had noticed several times before, that the backs of her hands were reminders that sun and weather had not passed gently by. She slipped meekly out of her blouse, turning her back to me in a gesture that clearly said she could not manage the tiny wire clasps of her bra without help. As I helped, it was as if my fingers were detached from the rest of me. We consciously avoided eye contact, systemic of the physical body syndrome and the family's lifelong decree, unwritten, unspoken, and unacknowledged, that we had bodies at all. At least, ones that could be seen by each other. Body parts, especially private ones, didn't exist in my family. That was the deal. However, this was a rare instance where that agreement had to be set aside. But even so, we were still held by the same old Nazarene demand for total and irrevocable modesty.

Her thin lips tightened and her breath came in little grunts as she slid her birdlike arms into the wide slits of the gown. We sat quietly waiting for the doctor, and she said, as I knew she would, "Burr. Kinda cold in here," a complaint that had nothing to do with the temperature but the mere thinness of the gown. By now I could read her mind. *Material this thin, I must be cold*, I could see her thinking. The women on her side of the family were always cold even when they weren't. They wore sweaters in the summer.

The doctor returned, made the routine check of basic vital signs. "Heart good, blood pressure perfect. Better than mine," chuckling, for our benefit I thought, which didn't amuse me. His presence was an irritation, but the way things were going, almost everything was. *Thump, thump thump thump, thump thump thump.* His fingertips tapped various parts of her bony, convex back. The stethoscope roamed the surface of her skin like the guide moving across a weathered Ouija board. As she leaned forward, the large armholes of the gown, loose and ill-fitting, fell open, and I could see part of her breast, long and flat and dangling, appearing tentatively attached to the concave hollow of her chest. Her back, bowl-shaped from arthritic distortion, was a cavity from which the stretches of skin hung nearly to her thighs, her torso assembled in its own convoluted logic. Sharp vertebrae insisted out from the center line of her back like knuckles in a clenched fist, the excess skin stretched transparently over each bone clinging like crepe that cascaded down her back in mottled tones of pink and gray. *Time sure fucks us up,* I said to myself. Tears welled in my eyes and grief pressed hard.

The exam was quick and perfunctory. I sensed the doctor had a spiel ready. He did, going directly to the point with the matter-of-fact conclusiveness the medical world matter-of-factly grants itself with authority that is almost an entitlement. "Well, guys, it's pretty clear."

"Guys" was too, too familiar and it wasn't the kind of address I'd heard from him before. Even with the lighthearted timbre in his voice, there was a detached bluntness that makes the truth go down hard and fast. This couldn't be good.

"Her body's telling us. It's shutting down. It can't, or rather won't, process food anymore. That's what this weight loss is all about. Not uncommon for someone her age. In her condition. The appetite stimulant we've had her on only fools the body for so long. It's been a couple of years now, hasn't it? But it's not working anymore. This is the body's way of exercising control in the only way it has left. It's saying no." Then he answered the question I wanted to ask before I could ask it, as if he'd read my mind.

"It's partly psychological. Partly not. We can't be one hundred percent sure. But we can't argue with what we do know. Can we do anything about it? Not much. A feeding tube. IVs to keep her hydrated. Some families want to go that route." I thought sarcastically, *As if they're planning a vacation?* What he was saying was for both of our benefits, Mom's and mine, but his eyes didn't divide their time and he looked only at me, directly into my eyes, as if my mother were not in the room. In her seat to the side of us, she sat in customary stoic diffidence with her eyes cast aside, fixed on nothing, listening but not hearing. I nodded slowly, blankly, to what he said, tried to digest what it would mean once we returned to the outside world beyond this small, antiseptic examination room. My stomach twisted into a knot, confirming what I couldn't quite bring myself to admit.

My eyes drifted out the window to the sycamore trees, deliquescent and staid. He kept talking but I had tuned the words out. In the sky, no migrating geese were flying yet. No disordered Vs, no plaintive honking. And the lives I might have led flashed by as I thought of the yellowing teeth I saw in the mirror every morning. I watched another gust of wind hurrying in circles. Green leaves bleeding yellow struggled to hold on to the branches. Some relinquished, let go. I felt a season not so much ending as one used up—like a love too much discussed or a desire too long deferred. Time had run out.

"You might think about hospice," the doctor continued, bringing me back into the present, his voice with no discernable sympathy, as if he were talking about the weather. And then, on an uplifted note, as if he were suggesting a new restaurant to try for lunch, "Is that something you've considered?"

"Well, no, not really." I had. Twice my mother had been in a nursing home and had dug her feet in, barking a rare display of resolution when we got her home: "Never again. Never again that stinky place. Promise me." The Davis woman in her was alive and well. The one of steel will. "I promise, Mom." End of subject.

The doctor continued, "You might want to. It's either that, or a nursing home, or round-the-clock home care, which gets pretty expensive, as you can imagine. Anyway, give it some thought and let me know. It doesn't have to be today. Soon, perhaps. I can set it up. I think it's time. Of course, it's up to you and your family."

And then directly to my mother as if she'd just entered the room, he said, "Marie, we've known you a long time. (*We* again! Good God! Now?) "You've been a good patient and an old friend." He got up as if we had just ended a weekly business meeting. He shook my hand. "Goodbye. Let me know what you want me to do." And as we left the office, "Next patient, Irene."

The hospice supervisor came to speak to us three days later. "It'd be better in the guest bedroom than in the master. Close to the larger bathroom. Easier to work out of." My brother and I took her suggestion to be a considerate observation and also a specific requirement.

This is how death inched its way into our lives, smoothly, almost an afterthought. There was no drama, no wringing of hands. Little increments of daily life changed. Modifications were made. Seamless adjustments. New became normal. The hospital bed arrived. And overnight, my brother and I set to transform the ordinary guest room into, if not a place grander, into a place less dreary. It was what we did best.

Decorating was our way of saying I love you without having to speak those three impossible words, words that were never uttered in our household. This simple affection, second nature, almost ordinary, in other families, was not accessible in ours. The simple phrase was the elephant in the room whose presence, while not in doubt, was as awkward as a piece of furniture that didn't fit anywhere and was better off ignored. The word *love* came from a far-off foreign place and stuck like a fine fish bone lodged in the throat. We did the best we could without it.

Material things were often the substitute, like lavish gifts at Christmas time, outrageous ones that had no practical application for how we lived—a mink coat for Mom, a red velvet smoking jacket for Dad. Extravagance equaled love. That was the translation. In this case, redoing the guest room, the last room our mother would inhabit, was one of those devices. A clear message of *I love you*, unspoken as always.

It was a small room in a typical three-bedroom, two-and-a-half-bath so-so subdivision house, quality taking second chair to the profit margin. Things we couldn't change, we had to ignore, like the cottage cheese ceiling and the brown, continent-shaped stain from a leak in the roof that hadn't been repainted after the old roof had been replaced; the hollow core closet doors that jumped off the track, nylon shag carpet, rust-colored, and a conglomerate of dissimilar furniture. We brought in a Chinese coromandel screen of dubious vintage from the living room and put it against the wall in back of the hospital bed, an incongruous coupling but the room's obvious focal point. We replaced the ceiling light, a flat, translucent square, with a small crystal chandelier from the hall, which left the electrical box there with live wires contorted downward, their stiff, short copper ends naked and hot.

Family photographs were the main accessory. We crammed the dresser with as many as would fit. The wedding picture of Mom's parents, Vess and Mae Davis, stood in the center, their sepia stares observing the decline of their last child, their three others residing at Sutter Memorial Cemetery just off the road to the Buttes, the small mountains of my high school Easter memory.

In one corner, a large gray combination safe, out of scale with the space it was in, became a table when we covered it with a sheet and crowded it with more photos. (My father always had a safe in the house. It was the symbol of the highly developed, inbred notion of Portuguese security and privacy, although I doubt that he thought of it that way. To him, a safe was as much a feature of any house we lived in as the kitchen sink or toilet.) When we put Mom to bed that first day, she scanned the room with blurred vision, nodding and smiling, her failing eyes pleased. It was then I noticed that she seemed to be growing smaller at a rate we could actually see.

The result was not what you'd see in the pages of *Architectural Digest*. Decorating on the cheap has limits. In spite of the lavender-scented candles, a faint smell of urine would creep in. Depends, too, have limits.

A dusty boom box from the garage sat on the floor near the only available wall plug, the other two inaccessible behind the big screen and the long dresser. The radio's bent antenna and weak signal faded in and out with more static than music and did not add the ambience we intended. Fresh flowers were arranged on the medical rolling swiveling table by the bed and another bouquet of artificial ones next to them, a gift from a distant niece in colors that made no sense. When all was said and done, the hospital bed with its snap-up rails and hydraulic lifts dominated the room. The superficiality of the trappings we so diligently arranged took nothing away from the one overriding truth: Mom was dying here.

Hospice arrived as scheduled, took over, and settled in with all professional assurance. Their supervision felt good, reassuring. Routine offered relief and a measure of security. But neither a pretty room nor a comforting routine changed the unalterable fact that at the end of every day, Mom's condition declined. She ate less at each meal, finally refusing to be fed with a spoon. "I'm not really very hungry today," was all she said. She lost the ability to hold a glass. Small sips of water or juice became problematic as her swallowing reflex weakened. Finally, an ice cube too small to choke on was her one source of hydration. Her urine changed color from light yellow to dark yellow to brown. "We need a catheter," Alma, the nurse, told me. "I'll bring one tomorrow. She'll be more comfortable."

Alma arrived late the next afternoon in her not-so-late model station wagon, the hood and roof faded to the prime coat. I watched her from the window over the kitchen sink, the lookout post I found myself lingering at for expected arrivals or a wished-for unscheduled visitor to give a break from the tedium of in-home health care. Days had gotten very long. The nurse's car was stacked high with medical supplies that looked like pressure-sealed passengers peeking out of the windows. The mirrored heat waves shimmied on the surface of the blacktop and roiled around her ankles as she hurried, clearly frazzled, across the street. I watched, wondering how it was humanly possible to keep up with the needs of all the dying. Alma was but one of thousands of hospice nurses scurrying around neighborhoods just like ours, mitigating death every day, helping people write themselves out of their own stories. Alma and all the nurses like her made up a virtual army, each soldier a Sisyphus in white polyester.

I opened the door just as she reached it, and she came across the threshold with an armful of supplies—in a sweat, overweight, good-natured, poured into tight-fitting synthetic pants and a top that by all rights should have been one or two sizes smaller. "Whew. That car's an oven! Air conditioner's on the fritz." Not a complaint, just a fact. None of the hospice staff ever seemed to complain. Astonishing, I thought. Alma got right to it.

"How's Mom doing? Okay?"

"Oh, about the same, I guess."

"Hmm. Okay, let's go see. Oh, by the way, this little procedure goes much smoother with two people. I mean, besides me and your mom, of course. Think you could give me a hand?"

She said this like I was being asked to help clear the table or fold clothes. Not that I hadn't anticipated the request. I had. I also had serious doubts that I could even be in the room when it happened but, "Yes, I can do it," is what I replied.

I followed Alma down the hall toward the bedroom, and my attention was drawn to her tiny feet, disproportionately small for her overall height and girth, and to the sound lilting up from bright white tennis shoes that squeaked almost timidly each time the rubber soles hit the tile floor. Her tight pants, too small for the thighs in them, rasped and hissed as she walked, and together with the sound of the shoes, created a cadence almost danceable. And-a-one-and-a-two.

"Hi, hon. How're we doin' today?" (The *we* thing again. Except coming from Alma, it had a different ring. She was clearly more emotionally invested.) Mom's response was a weak smile, barely a smile at all, just quivering lips. "Okay, well," Alma continued, "we're gonna fix ya up good today. We're gonna git rid of those chucks once and for all, okay? You'll be a lot more comfortable. Easier for you, too," she said, and winked at me.

Mom stared at her, not understanding anything that had been said. Alma, the picture of efficiency, wasted no time. "Let's just get this old thing off. Okay?" She peeled the Velcro back from both sides of the adult diaper and in half the time it took me had it off and in the brown paper waste bag on the floor by the bed.

"No more depending on Depends!" she giggled.

Depends! What an insipid name, I thought. *Depends on what? Depends on if there is someone to change them for you! That's what it depends on.* Even coming from June Allison's sweet mouth, a film star of my mother's era who had prostituted herself (too unkind?) to doing a television ad for the product, the name still sounded stupid. But the bottom line is always the bottom line. June Allison. Did she actually wear those things herself?

Alma gave me a nod. My cue. I raised Mom's left knee up gently with one hand, as high as possible against the resistance of stiff joints. A flashlight Alma had given me was in my other hand. "Shine it right in there," she said nodding in that direction, as she lifted mom's right knee, gently but dispassionately, like an auto mechanic lifting the hood of a vintage car. "Down and a little to the right. Right in there," she said. The moment had come. From a vantage point the likes of which no son should ever see, I stared at my mother's ninety-three-year-old vagina—that mysterious and private part that was always hidden and now completely exposed, wincing self-consciously. Or was this idea a figment of the imagination because of how completely mortified I was? It didn't matter. One thing was certain. There was no backing out now. No hole to crawl into. Turning away was not an option.

Horrified, I stared blankly at a naked and spent body part, a rise of stubble on a worn-out landscape that in youth was as moist as a pink, sticky-pedaled hibiscus but now a decaying *cattleya*, dry and purplish brown amid the gray pallor of clinging skin settling nervously around the curves. It pulsed slightly and looked up at me as I looked down at it. I saw the end of summer-dead grass, fallen husks, and parched earth, and for some reason, I was both detached and invested, staring into the ancient apex, the cradle of man, the crux of all possibility, a bloom dying, decomposing, and returning to the soil, nature's slow, inevitable revenge on every garden.

Her stiff legs jutted in awkward angles. I took a deep breath. *I can do this,* I said to myself, even as the walls started closing in. Old faces from the dresser stared—some out of curiosity, some in disbelief. Alma hovered and I stood rigid at my post, ill-prepared. The enemy was fortified, the curved mound defiant.

Alma remained confident and relaxed. This was routine stuff. She lubed her surgically gloved fingers with K-Y jelly and slathered a generous amount on and in the quivering genitalia, her fingers massaging, relaxing, trying to alleviate the tenseness. The reaction, however, was a warning shot. ATTENTION! ALERT! INTRUDER!

"This feels good, doesn't it, hon, okay?"

I felt sick, revolted, embarrassed for myself and for my mother, her cloudy eyes gazing toward the cottage cheese. The angry vagina was highly agitated, in revolt, wincing and recoiling like a snail into its shell.

Alma reassured her. "Don't worry, honey. Everything's gonna be okay. Okay?" The bad feeling I had had grown worse.

Staring out the bedroom window as she applied the gel, Alma's eyes blinked in syncopated time, seemingly detached from what her hands were doing, as if her fingers had little minds of their own and were devising their own strategies. "Where should I go now? How far should I push? A little to the left. Higher. Now lower, then up, then in. No. Not there," a conversation I imagined they were having. Alma blinked as if to a metronome, and when she felt the time had come, her eyes turned back to the project, brows furrowed with question, and said muttering to herself, "Okay. Let's give it a try." She picked up a length of thin plastic tubing and began easing it into the opening, which was tense and quivering.

"Okay, you're gonna feel a little pressure and then a tiny pinprick. That's all. Okay?" My mother's confused face stared up blankly from the pillow, having no concept of what was happening. "Down a little and to the right with the light," she said to me. As close to nausea as I was, I couldn't look away. I adjusted the beam. The catheter slid cautiously in. "Okay, it'll just last a second. No. Don't tense up," she said assertively. "It won't work if you fight it. Just relax, hon, now don't tense up. Okay?"

The flexible tube slid a few centimeters in and then stopped abruptly, curling back on itself. At that moment, my mother's body arched up in a contortion, as if she had received a jolt of electricity. She threw her head back. Her throat muscles constricted. Arthritic bamboo fingers clenched the bed sheet and her mouth shaped itself into a silent scream, as if it was trapped in a jar. From chin to collarbone, striations of ligament and veins popped as if they would burst through the thin layer of skin. Then pain found a voice.

"OW! OH, NO. OWWWW, THAT HUUURTS! NO!"

My stomach leapt into my throat. *I'm going to be sick! Steady. Hold steady. Breathe.* Temporary fadeout. The house across the street. Bobby. Click. Like a camera.

"C'mon, buddy. Relax. Almost. It's almost in. It'll be okay. Just relax. Okay?"

"Ouch. OW! Stop it!"

"C'mon. Try. Try one more time. Relax! Relax and it won't hurt. I can't get it in if you're tense." The cage is still there.

I yelled into the pillow. *"OWW! NO! IT HURTS!"* He pulled out what little that was in me, grabbed a Kleenex from the nightstand, and wiped what looked like peanut butter from the tip of his penis.

"Shit! Jesus, don't you wipe?"

"Course," I said, mortified, staring at the pillow, red rising in my neck. I was mad, embarrassed. "It hurts! You push too hard!"

Click. I was back.

Alma was calm, miraculously so. She eased the tube out.

"Thank God," I said out loud, heaving a sigh of relief. But it wasn't over.

"Oh, honey, I'm so sorry. Okay?" She whispering to herself, "I don't think this is going to work." But to me, "We'll try once more. She's just so tight, though. Lots of atrophy in there, and I'm hitting scar tissue, I think. Maybe there's a way around. Sometimes there is."

Then, smiling, she said to Mom, "Okay. Honey. I'm going to try one more time. I know this isn't fun, but just try to relax a little. Okay? Your life will be so much easier if I can get this in." She glanced at me, forced a smile, which curled down into a frown, and turned back toward my mother. "One more try. The old college try," as if a cliché would make a difference. "She'll be so much better off if we can this darn thing in." She bent back down, repositioned the tube, and barely touched the skin.

"NO! GOD, THAT HURTS! IT HUUURTS! STOP! PLEEEASE! NO MORE! I CAN'T TAKE ANYMORE!"

"It's no use. No go. This is not gonna work. Okay, we're done, sweetie. Okay?" She rolled the tubing loosely and tossed it into the brown bag of waste on the floor by the bed while she gathered up the other paraphernalia, babbling on about this and that, kvetching about her workload. To me, what had happened was a mind-blowing, retching, catastrophic fiasco of monumental proportion. To Alma, just another day at the office. Failure was no one's fault in the world of hospice, just one setback among many. All in the course of any given day.

"Darn. I'm running so late. Two of the visiting nurses are on vacation this week, another one is out sick, and we're so backed up. I won't get home till nine or ten tonight." The litany of pleasantries came next, the ones on the tail end of every visit—how well Mom looked, how pretty, how nice the room smelled.

While I listened, I straightened Mom's legs, still stranded in a confused contortion. I covered her back up with the bedding and thought, *I was born breech. No wonder she almost died.* The knot clenched in the pit of my gut had produced stomach acid that pushed its way up to my throat. Mom's hollow eyes continued to scan the ceiling, looking at nothing, from a place in time neither forward nor backward. Dementia was in this instance a friend, a welcome thief, erasing the intolerable and already-forgotten experience. Not for the first time, nor the last, I wondered if I would be this lucky, if luck is what dementia can ever be called. Would life's last indignities be canceled out for me, as they were for her? Would I, too, be impossible to catheterize, staring vacuously at some synthetic ceiling somewhere? Would another caregiver, one like Alma, a virtual stranger, be my last and only caregiver?

"You'll have to keep changing her, I'm afraid."

"I don't mind," I replied. "I've gotten so used to doing it. Wish I was better at it."

We walked down the hall.

"Still having bowel movements, is she?"

"Some. Not much. She's not eating. A few bites, maybe."

"Just a little smear, like, on the chuck?"

Jesus! Don't you wipe?

"Uh-huh."

"That's normal. Still givin' her some liquids?"

"Yes."

"Good. Keep her hydrated as much as possible, okay?"

"Okay."

The melody of her shoes and thighs played on the tile, but this time the steps were slower—a dirge, not a dance. "Well, I'll see you in two days. Sooner, if you need. Remember. Call if there's a big change or if anything worries you. Anything at all. We'll send someone right over. We want her to be as comfortable as possible. There are things we can still do. You're doing a great job, okay? I wish we had a hundred like you."

As she grabbed the doorknob to leave, I stammered, as my mother would have when she was unsure of what she was about to say, and asked the question I found myself asking each hospice member as they left the house. "How long . . . do you think?" Each time answered with different responses—guarded and benevolently vague.

"Probably only days at this point."

"No one can tell for sure."

"I've never seen it go for more than three weeks. And that's unusual."

"You just never know."

"Just keep doin' what you're doing'. You're doing a great job. I wish we had a hundred like you," she repeated.

"Yes. Thank you. I will."

I closed the door behind the nurse and stood in the entrance hall thinking how different my life is compared to how I dreamed it would be or might have been. Thoughts stretched back and forth—then, now—and fragments piled one on top of the other, some in detail, some in shards: How I came to embrace my heritage. What I learned to recognize in the *fado* voices—the *saudade* of my forefathers, my paternal family, and myself. How it all made sense now that I had put to rest many of the preoccupations that had troubled me, disciplined them away to a sensible place. They were not part of real life as real life had turned out, in the same way that the cage of monkeys evolved into the cage of life.

I sat in the living room and let faces and the experiences attached to them wing by like hummingbirds pausing midair, trembling, or childhood doubts that are not done with me, nor will they ever be.

Likewise, the relationships from long ago that are woven into the fabric of my experience are so far back in time I try to convince myself I am finished with them when I am not. In truth, echoing Virginia Woolf, "But though they are gone, the night is full of them." Bobby, whose face has finally blurred. And Jack, whose face hasn't; Betty, and a spin-the-bottle kiss that rocked our worlds. We laughed together, danced together, and were romantic off and on through high school. She was my first puppy love. She's gone. And Laurie, whose name comes up at the end. *Why now?* I have to ask myself. I suppose it's because she was better than the book. This book, anyway. She was the one I almost married, even as those voices screamed, "Don't do it," and I did her the favor of walking away, knowing I could never have been an honest or faithful husband. Her name and picture appeared in the obituary column of the newspaper not so very long ago. I bookmarked it, as I did Jack's.

So, you see, a life can never be told in one telling.

In some ways the people I've written about, as well as the ones I've failed to mention, are more real to me now than they were then. Their stars burn brighter. I see them, and myself, through clearer eyes, as, one by one, they depart like the players off the stage in Haydn's "Farewell" Symphony. It is not sad, since, in its mysterious way, aging conditions you to accept loss. Collectively, they taught me love is not always what it seems. There are desires that love cannot satisfy, ones that can never be satisfied.

The others? The ones I remember but no longer think of except to wonder from time to time, *Do they ever think of me, as I have them? And then the final questions, When will my name be spoken for the last time? When will I no longer be anywhere in anyone's memory?*

Laurie Michaels, circa 1958.

I am the elderly man I never thought I would be, still viable in certain ways but no longer dressing to please or shaving every day. I cry more now and easily, even though I don't have a lot to cry about.

But a television commercial can produce immediate tears, like the one with the woeful looking dogs and cats in cold cages and the plaintive voice. "Some animals will be left abandoned in the freezing weather tonight. Won't you help with a donation?" A song can do it too. Or just seeing another old person and thinking, *There I am*. It's ironic. I'm told I cried incessantly, inexplicably, when I was a baby. That my very young mother would pace the floor with me in her arms screaming at the top of my lungs. "Please, Richie, please," she'd plead, "please don't cry, please don't. What's the matter? What's wrong?" And then when I was older, a teenager, a young adult, I rarely cried at all even though so many times I wanted to.

Now I sigh weighted sighs I never could have imagined and go along with life as it continues in its ineffable way to manufacture memories. I find pleasure in remembering, although there is something about sharing it this way that feels invasive. I'm not sure why, except perhaps that it forces me to face, once and for all, the artifice and imperfection I've tried to discard. And am showing it to you. But then, is there anything artificial or imperfect in matters of the heart?

Reaching back in time is innocent when you're old. And it's easier to edit out the disturbing edges of the past. Those that remain are soft, like the after tone of a tuning fork, struck but still resonating. Much remains in the margins of a life, much at the edges, not a part of any narrative. Some things are imperfectly preserved in what was wrongly described by someone as "the clear amber of memory."

Part of me still wonders why I write this. Is it so that I am not completely, irretrievably, irreversibly irrelevant and invisible in the way that most old people are? I try to think that my resignation of age is less than cynical, even laced with a touch of humor. I do find a little comfort in accepting my own insignificance, a thought that calms me, and vexes me too. And there is still the underlying question: How many pages have I embellished memories with what I wanted, needed them to be? And if I've done that, isn't it not so much an inaccuracy as it is a romance, a reality seen in a certain light? With the dismissiveness that humor affords, is any of this of any use now? Or is it just dust blown in your face by the wind? The unalterable truth is, when I am gone, these thoughts will all displace and disassemble into a diminishing ether. In fact, haven't they already?

I walked back to the bedroom to check on my mother. She was not asleep, not awake. Long intervals were the spaces between each breath—little stopping places, pauses that bought more time. It was as if the next breath was a matter of deciding. Soft rattles, whispering. I leaned over and kissed her softly on the forehead, my lips barely touching the skin. "I love you, Mom," I said quietly, but out loud, for the first time in my life, the words not feeling foreign at all, as if I had said I love you to her a million times. She lay there in a semiconscious state, took another deep breath and said whisperingly, "Ai . . . uv . . . ou . . . too." She sighed and fell into a deeper state—sleep, or an approximation of sleep, beneath the flow of time closer and closer to that place where the first and last moment of your life meet, compressing into nothing.

I sat down in the living room, thinking how grateful I am for all I have in life and how little I've compromised how I've become who I am. And, finally, how lucky I am for the longtime relationship with Chris I am now securely wrapped in.

I picked up the book lying on the coffee table: Truman Capote's *A Christmas Memory*. I make a habit of rereading this magical little story every cold Christmas morning, very early, with a hot cup of coffee and the stillness of the faint predawn light coming in the window. I feel the need to read it now. The story is so familiar, but as many times as I have read it, I am never able to repress quiet tears when, at the end, Queenie is buried with her bone in Simpson's field and Buddy looks up at the winter sky searching for kites hurrying toward heaven. Only this time it's the last few pages I turn to, thinking how many of my references lately turn to the past. Have I become too old to belong in the present, where nothing is like it was and never will be? Will, in the very last breath I breathe, Bobby or Jack or Betty or Laurie or anyone come back to me as figures sometimes do in the end, wanting some final attention for having had me in their lives? And, as always, the trinity of experience ends with another question. Yesterday. Today. Tomorrow?

I put the book down and walked to the kitchen thinking how glad I would be when the summer was finally gone and that time between seasons comes, the small window of calm that opens before the heavy rains and shrieking wind fill the days and weeks and months until buds swell again. I stood at the kitchen sink remembering a notion I'd read or heard somewhere that a person doesn't really become an adult until they lose both parents. Was that true, I wondered?

Out the window and down the street, I looked to where the sky stopped before it should, where roofs and treetops held it back. I leaned against the sink and turned on the tap, breaking the silence I shared with the rest of the house. The water smelled of sulfur.

Yuba City water always did and probably always would. Some things don't change. I dwelled on the notion about one's parents, that thing about becoming an adult. I tried to recall something but then couldn't remember what it was, something that I'd held close and caused a flutter but that I couldn't summon. And, for a second, I had to think twice about why I still wore white gym socks to bed. But then I remembered.

THE END

Gomukhasana pose, 2019.

ACKNOWLEDGMENTS

Bear Rowell, much to my resistance and disbelief, informed me years ago that I was a writer before I ever thought I might be. She encouraged the lengthy, painful, early drafts of this book and was always there with eager, constructive feedback.

I was supported, pushed, and cajoled by a long list of people who offered their help and expertise in various forms—all of which I consider editing. My good friend Karen Randall gave me early counsel and direction; Wendy Roscher provided technical editorial coordination and improvement; the editors Julianne Couch, David Ferris, and David Aretha helped me fine-tune the paragraphs, sentences, and words.

And finally, the excellent Cadence Group put the pages into a polished, professional production with Kim Bookless adding the final editorial touches and Bethany Brown coordinating the entire process. Thanks also to David Carriere, who then created and steered publicity where it needed to go.

No acknowledgment would be complete without a final and affectionate nod to all those in my life who made up the experiences from which I drew the memories. Each contributed to the reimagining of my history. The main ones followed me like shadows or haunted me like ghosts, and, to rephrase one thought from the Prologue, each deserves more attention than I have given them. They made my life more confusing, more difficult, and ultimately richer, fuller, and more exultant than it would have been without them. And that by revisiting ". . . a stone, a leaf, an unfound door, . . ." I found that I could, in the moment, go home again, learning that going back is often going forward.